ORTHO'S All About

Creating
Natural
Landscapes

Meredith® Books
Des Moines, Iowa

D1122213

Ortho® Books
An imprint of Meredith® Books

All About Creating Natural Landscapes
Project Editors: Michael MacCaskey, Lynn Ocone
Editor: Denny Schrock
Contributing Editors: Marilyn Rogers, Michael D. Smith
Contributing Technical Editors: Margaret Livingston, Joetta
  Miller, Sally Roth
Contributing Writer: Eric Clough
Senior Associate Design Director: Tom Wegner
Assistant Editor: Harijs Priekulis
Copy Chief: Terri Fredrickson
Copy and Production Editor: Victoria Forlini
Editorial Operations Manager: Karen Schirm
Managers, Book Production: Pam Kvitne,
  Marjorie J. Schenkelberg
Contributing Copy Editor: Sharon McHaney
Contributing Proofreaders: Mary Duerson, Elise Marton,
  Karen Schultz
Contributing Map Illustrator: Jana Fothergill
Indexer: Ellen Davenport
Electronic Production Coordinator: Paula Forest
Editorial and Design Assistants: Kathleen Stevens, Karen
  McFadden

**Additional Editorial Contributions from
  Art Rep Services**
Director: Chip Nadeau
Designers: lk Design, Gary Hespenheide
Illustrators: Dave Brandon, Rick Hanson, Shawn Wallace

Meredith® Books
Editor in Chief: Linda Raglan Cunningham
Design Director: Matt Strelecki
Executive Editor, Gardening and Home Improvement:
  Benjamin W. Allen
Executive Editor, Gardening: Michael McKinley

Publisher: James D. Blume
Executive Director, Marketing: Jeffrey Myers
Executive Director, New Business Development:
  Todd M. Davis
Executive Director, Sales: Ken Zagor
Director, Operations: George A. Susral
Director, Production: Douglas M. Johnston
Business Director: Jim Leonard

Vice President and General Manager: Douglas J. Guendel

Meredith Publishing Group
President, Publishing Group: Stephen M. Lacy
Vice President-Publishing Director: Bob Mate

Meredith Corporation
Chairman and Chief Executive Officer: William T. Kerr

Chairman of the Executive Committee: E.T. Meredith III

All of us at Ortho® Books are dedicated to providing you
with the information and ideas you need to enhance your
home and garden. We welcome your comments and
suggestions about this book. Write to us at:
  Meredith Corporation
  Ortho Gardening Books
  1716 Locust St.
  Des Moines, IA 50309–3023

If you would like to purchase any of our gardening, home
improvement, cooking, crafts, or home decorating and design
books, check wherever quality books are sold. Or visit us at:
meredithbooks.com

If you would like more information on other Ortho products,
call 800-225-2883 or visit us at: www.ortho.com

Thanks to
Spectrum Communication Services, Inc., Mary Irene Swartz

Photographers
  (Photographers credited may retain copyright ©
  to the listed photographs.)
L = Left, R = Right, C = Center, B = Bottom, T = Top

Ian Adams/gardenIMAGE: 84B; **Margarite
Bradley/Positive Images:** 38R; **Gay Bumgarner:** 91R;
Gay Bumgarner/Positive Images: 7BR, 9T, 10TL;
Christi Carter: 13T, 16B, 20B, 23B, 26B, 30TR, 38L;
David Cavagnaro: 84CR; **Carolyn Chatterton:** 82R,
Candace Cochrane/Positive Images: 21; **Crandall &
Crandall:** 58, 59TL, 70C; **R. Todd Davis:** 27, 42B, 50TR,
54; **Richard Day/Daybreak Imagery:** 9B, 19T, 32B, 80C,
83, 84TR, 85T, 89B; **Alan Detrick:** 69L; **Michael Dirr:**
42T, 44T; **Christine M. Douglas:** 8B, 14B, 78; **Catriona
Tudor Erler:** 62T; **Derek Fell:** 10B, 16T, 36L, 55B;
Susan M. Glascock: 36; **John Glover:** 34B, 39R, 55TR,
59TR; **David Goldberg:** 68B; **Harry Haralambou/Positive
Images:** 57B; **Margaret Hensel/Positive Images:** 11T;
Saxon Holt: 3L-6, 74B, 81T; **Jerry Howard/Positive
Images:** 8T, 12T, 14T; **Bernard Jackson:** 85B; **Bill Johnson:**
25B, 52L, 87T; **Don Johnston; Photo/Nats:** 22T;
Jim Kahnweiler/Positive Images: 7T; **Rosemary Kautzky:**
3L-3, 46, 47BL, 48, 49B, 50TL, 51L, 90B; **Pete Krumhardt:**
49TR; **Andrew Lawson:** 36CR, 45C, 52R; **Scott Leonhart/
Positive Images:** 91L; **David Liebman:** 80B, 86T, 89T;
Janet Loughrey: 6T, 13B; **Stephen G. Maka; Photo/Nats:**
18TR; **Allan Mandell:** 12B; **Charles Mann:** 30B;
David McDonald: 66T, 67T; **Charles Melton:** 19B, 22B,
81B; **Clive Nichols:** 56B; **Steven Nikkila:** 53, 65T, 90T;
Jerry Pavia: 3L-2, 28; **Cheryl R. Richter:** 20T; **Gregory K.
Scott:** 11B, 82L, 88; **Julie Maris/Semel:** 7BL; **Richard
Shiell:** 3L-1, 4, 39L, 42C, 85C; **Pam Spaulding/Positive
Images:** 6B, 24B, 45T; **Joseph G. Strauch Jr.:** 40T;
Michael Thompson: 87B; **Connie Toops:** 86B; **Mark
Turner:** 15, 25T; **Lee Anne White/Positive Images:** 18L

On the cover: Drifts of threadleaf coreopsis (*Coreopsis
verticillata* 'Moonbeam'), black-eyed Susan (*Rudbeckia hirta*),
common rose mallow (*Hibiscus moscheutos* 'Caroline'),
purple coneflower (*Echinacea purpurea*), and several varieties
of daylilies (*Hemerocallis* spp.) combine with kousa dogwood
(*Cornus kousa*) to create a colorful naturalistic foreground
for this Midwestern vista. Photo by Alise O'Brien.

Note to the Readers: Due to differing conditions, tools,
and individual skills, Meredith Corporation assumes no
responsibility for any damages, injuries suffered, or losses
incurred as a result of following the information published
in this book. Before beginning any project, review the
instructions carefully, and if any doubts or questions remain,
consult local experts or authorities. Because codes and
regulations vary greatly, you always should check with
authorities to ensure that your project complies with all
applicable local codes and regulations. Always read and
observe all of the safety precautions provided by
manufacturers of any tools, equipment, or supplies,
and follow all accepted safety procedures.

NATURE'S INTRICATE WEBS 4

THE REGIONS AND PLANTS OF NORTH AMERICA 14

NATURAL GARDENS IN ARID REGIONS 26

NATURAL GARDENS IN HUMID REGIONS 38

PONDS AND POND MAKING 54

PLANTS & PLANTING 68

ENCOURAGING WILDLIFE 80

NATURE'S INTRICATE WEBS

Sunflowers, phlox, asters, and coneflowers in this meadow landscape provide nectar for butterflies and seeds for birds.

The fabric of nature is complex and mysterious. Smaller webs of life function within myriad others. As a tree is a fully functioning system itself, it is also part of a forest. And the forest is a working system which is part of a still larger system. All of life is part of a larger whole.

For much of history, people have struggled to impose some sort of order on nature. The agrarian settlers of North America carved farms from the wilderness and maintained them only by contending with nature.

But now there is a greater understanding of our place in nature and a deeper awareness of ecology. Gardeners, especially, are beginning to understand how intimately their gardens are connected to the local community and to the world beyond.

Landscaping nature's way is good for the environment. Such gardens require less water, less support from pesticides and fertilizers, and they require less work to maintain. Moreover, they'll likely encourage local birds, butterflies, and animals to return. After all, why travel to natural areas when you can have it out your own back door?

THE NATURAL LANDSCAPING IDEA IS NOT NEW

During the Renaissance, people viewed nature as a force they needed to dominate and control. The formal garden—the imposition of a pattern on nature—was conceived and remained prevalent through the industrial revolution. Classical gardens were seen as works of geometry and symmetry, the product of the rational mind. The Renaissance gardens of Italy featured an axis down the center that divided the garden into two balanced halves. The French extended this design with multiple axes and complex woven patterns. The palace gardens of Versailles and Vaux le Vicomte are the culmination of this style. Civilization's conquering of nature was glorified, with the universe as a precise and perfectly functioning machine as the inspiration. Many gardens are still patterned on this philosophy of design.

The Japanese garden represents another way of viewing a partnership with nature. It is a carefully designed symbolic representation of nature, incorporating humans as an integral part of the greater whole. The garden is neither pure nature nor an artificial creation; it is a work of art that captures the essence of nature rather than duplicating it. A group of carefully placed stones might represent mountains. In another context they might represent islands in a vast and peaceful sea. Some Japanese gardens are abstracted; others are soft, literal representations. Their common ground is a respect for nature.

Natural landscaping is also founded on tradition. In the 18th century, landscape designer Capability Brown redesigned the English landscape by creating a master plan for the community's common area. This was essentially a diverse meadowland designed in full cooperation with natural ecological processes, a place for people living in a sustainable community with other creatures. Domestic and wild animals shared the common grazing land and the woodlands. People and their gardens inhabited the edges. Brown's comprehensive plan allowed for process and evolution.

Numerous insects, large and small, depend upon the nectar of flowers for sustenance. Here a honeybee sips from a verbena floret.

Woodland parks form the heart of many cities in the United States. New York's Central Park, the core of the city, is a naturalized woodland with a diverse wildlife community. Although only a small percentage of the trees, shrubs, and other plants growing there are native, all of the plants are adapted to the site. Except for the lawn areas and display beds, the plantings require little maintenance. Likewise, portions of Golden Gate Park in San Francisco are also almost fully naturalized. In fact, most large cities in North America incorporate generous park areas based on a naturalized design.

Support the birds, butterflies, and beneficial insects that visit your garden by providing as wide a variety of blooming plants as possible. Here various native and nativelike plants produce a colorful show as well as meals for friendly visitors.

CREATING NATURAL GARDENS

Perennials planted in drifts, rather than rows, give this garden a dynamic, natural appearance. High-summer blossoms include yellow yarrow, orange lilies, and purple salvias.

Blooming phlox and wild violets spilling into the pathway soften the hard look of landscape ties and link the pathway with surrounding plantings.

Every region has its own possibilities for natural gardens. But rather than copy nature, try to learn from your local environment. This book describes the basics of how to create a natural garden that is right for your particular region.

The key to a natural garden is adapting the attitude of a natural landscape. Such an approach works in any region in North America. To start, consider four key principles:

■ Natural rather than artificial materials
■ Curving, irregular lines rather than straight or sharp-angled corners
■ A flow of plants in naturalistic groupings rather than individual specimens
■ Layered plantings with groundcovers, flowers, shrubs, and trees

You may notice new additions that you did not plant; some will be weeds, some native plants, and some volunteers from other gardens or your own. You could take a wait-and-see approach with the weeds. Many are opportunists, adapted to colonizing disturbed areas quickly. Remove these aggressive, weedy plants as soon as they appear.

Although a natural gardener interferes as little as possible in nature's trial and error approach, this is after all your yard. So interfere but carefully, understanding how to tip the balance in one direction or another. Remove plants you dislike and limit the growth of those that threaten to take over.

Crevices in lichen-covered rocks are home to pink-flowered phlox. The use of a single kind of stone and a low-growing perennial that appears to tumble about gives the garden a realistic, natural appearance.

This pond looks natural even though it was planted by a gardener. It's an ideal attraction for a wide variety of wildlife and a great spot for fish.

Asters, goldenrod, sumac, maiden grass, and mums achieve full glory in the fall garden. Here they intertwine in layered plantings to create a natural-looking garden.

LETTING NATURE DO IT

You can work with nature to create your own natural garden. If you enter into a working partnership and dialogue with nature, it will do most of the work. Nature provides the sun, the water, most of the fertilizer, weed and insect control, and the plants too.

Nature balances with diversity. It abounds in plants, insects, amphibians, reptiles, mammals, and birds that interact with each other, creating a community with its own unique characteristics and balance. For example, today's mature oak tree grew from an acorn, which may have been placed by a squirrel at least a century ago. Regional influences such as soil and weather also affect these interactions. So does human intervention. A maple seedling might be crushed by a flying baseball or aided by a fertilizer pellet. The branch of science that studies these communities and interactions is called ecology, from the Latin for "the study of households."

Nature works within a complex set of natural laws. The interactions governed by these laws are often subtle and delicate. The seeds of sun-loving plants will not sprout in dense shade. Plants needing lots of water will grow around a pond, not in a dry meadow. By understanding how these natural laws operate in your own yard, you can cooperate with nature.

CHANGE IN NATURE

Just as nature uses diversity to maintain a balance, it also uses it to produce change. The inevitability of change is one of the

In the grip of change, an abandoned apple orchard that once favored fruit production for people now nurtures a variety of plants and animals.

Ring-necked pheasants forage in open gardens with nearby cover—such as brush piles, briar patches, or trees—that offers protection for nighttime roosting.

exciting and magical aspects of natural gardening. Time does not stand still; your garden evolves as you live and work with it. This evolution is called succession.

Succession can be rapid or slow. If you stop mowing your lawn, it can become a meadow quite quickly. It will take much longer for the meadow to become a woodland. You can speed up or slow down the natural process of succession, cocreating with nature instead of fighting with it, and at the same time enjoying the various wildlife communities in the changing environment.

A trim lawn can become a meadow. The shrubs and trees that sprout in it become part of the evolving community. Birds like the cover and find food in the meadow. As the trees grow, squirrels and birds move in. As the branches die, the dead wood becomes a home to borers and carpenter ants, and woodpeckers find food and shelter in them.

DIVERSITY IN NATURE

When you visit natural areas with a range of environmental conditions, you will notice an accompanying range of communities. One of them might be a mature forest. Its dense shade limits the types of plants and animals that can live there. An open woodland, with more sun and brighter shade, can host a wider variety of plants, animals, and insects. Just as a mature forest has less diversity than an open woodland, likewise a shady garden hosts a smaller range of plants than a sunny garden.

Forest edge habitat occurs at the boundaries between different types of land cover. Some species require edge habitat, such as birds that nest in forests and forage in nearby fields.

Meadows, too, have a wide variety of plants and animals. Wildflowers burst forth in spring and fall, joining the meadow's many perennial plants, intriguing groupings of shrubs, and dramatic and interesting grasses.

Streams running through forests and meadows attract additional types of plants and animals. Amphibians, crustaceans, water insects, and sometimes fish live here. Ferns are prolific. Raccoons and other animals frequent the area to feed on aquatic creatures.

A planted meadow (top) that appears quite natural includes butterfly weed, black-eyed Susan, Queen Anne's lace, and larkspur. Songbirds (above), such as this American goldfinch, are drawn to the ripening seeds of many meadow perennials, including purple coneflower.

USING NATURE AS YOUR GUIDE

When you decide to comanage your property with nature as a partner, you adopt the role of steward, artistic director, and trustee. Landscaping with nature means giving up some control. It is a courageous experiment and an act of faith in nature's process. The steward's role is unique for each garden.

Here's how to be a garden steward.

Gone are lawn and neatly trimmed shrubs in this Pacific Northwest garden. In their place, shrubs find their natural form and combine with water to create a woodland habitat welcoming to visiting creatures.

Blanket flowers (above) are among the many wildflowers that require less water and maintenance than lawn. A pond (right) hosts an abundance of wildlife. Water plants provide food for water fowl, floating plants serve as landing pads for insects, and the rocky edge gives amphibians hibernation spots.

Ponds attract amphibians, including frogs and toads that help keep insect pests in check.

Thinning branches of large trees allow light to pass through the canopy to the ground, which means that flowering plants, such as these spring-blooming primroses, can thrive.

REDUCE WATERING: In the West where rainfall is naturally low, many common landscape plants are unfortunately adapted to chronic overwatering from sprinklers. Gradually reduce the amount of landscape water you use until it approaches what is normal for your region. Use your irrigation system only to supplement rainfall during prolonged drought.

Some plants will suffer from reduced watering. Transplant them to a corner of the garden you intend to water, or give them away. Replace these with plants that are more in keeping with reduced irrigation.

MOW HIGH, LESS OFTEN: You could mow the lawn only once in fall, to simulate the effects of a prairie fire. Scatter seeds of a few wildflowers that are native to your area. Specialty seed growers have wildflower selections for each of the major regions.

STOP SHEARING HEDGES: Shearing forms a dense, twiggy cluster at the ends of the plant stems, making hedges nearly impenetrable by most birds, thereby preventing nesting. If pruning is necessary, do it selectively with hand shears.

CREATE AREAS OF EXPOSED WATER: Wildlife needs and appreciates water. It can be in the form of a natural pond, birdbath, garden stream, or waterfall. Water can make your garden a favorite place for wildlife to visit or to live, but keep it circulating to avoid pests such as mosquitos.

THIN OUT EXISTING TREES: If your existing tree canopy is dense and casts heavy shade, open up the canopy with selective thinning. Light and air encourage undergrowth and appeal to a wider variety of birds and other wildlife.

Rabbits may visit your garden if you provide cover. Brush piles and dense thickets of unpruned shrubs, especially those with thorns, offer the shelter they prefer. Rabbits feed on buds, leaves, berries, and tender tips of twigs.

PLANNING A NATURAL GARDEN

An arid garden, like the desert it mimics, has exposed soil and plants widely spaced. Native stones positioned among plants add authenticity.

Trees planted in this Pacific Northwest garden appear to be growing naturally.

Although "planning" and "natural" may seem to be opposed concepts, your garden will be more satisfying if it is planned. This planning, however, should acknowledge and accommodate nature's own sense of style.

Trees in natural woodland settings are most often found in clusters or groups, rarely as individual specimens. Repeat this pattern in your garden for a more natural appearance. Plant screens of trees or shrubs to hide unpleasant views and create privacy. Use trees to block the wind. Leave some open spaces between background trees for interest, and avoid planting tall species in locations that will block your—or your neighbors'— view of pleasant vistas or sunsets. Some drought-resistant trees are interesting and effective shade trees. Use a small individual shade tree to create a canopy over your patio or deck.

In dry woodlands the ground under trees is frequently bare or only sparsely covered. The plants compete vigorously for the scarce water by lacing their shallow roots through as much soil as possible. Dense tree roots prevent other plants from growing too close. Some trees actually release toxins to prevent the growth of other plants, which would compete for water and available nutrients. When you design your garden, decide whether to leave bare or mulched earth in places or cover all the ground with plants. Although dense plantings may not look natural, they help prevent the growth of weeds.

Avoid overplanting trees and shrubs. Space them far enough apart so they will not be crowded when they mature. Plants in arid conditions need lots of room to get enough nutrients and water. Plant annual wildflowers or temporary perennials as fill-in material until your permanent plantings have gained their mature size.

To create a feeling of continuity and rhythm, repeat these groupings with varying arrangements throughout the garden. Although variety is important for interest and diversity, many natural landscapes consist of only a few species repeated in an ever-changing interplay of patterns. You can mass together a limited number of native perennials and wildflowers to form stunning drifts of color.

SHAPING THE LAND

Before you plant your garden, make structural changes to the land to make it more useful and more interesting. Shaping and sculpting the soil into hills and mounds is an option whether you live on a hill or your property is flat. If you enjoy exercise, a shovel and a wheelbarrow are the only tools you need. Or you can use a small garden tractor for minor grading changes to transform the character of your land. Use the earth you excavate for a pond to make a mound.

Nonplant features in the landscape add interest whether the landscape design is traditional or follows the patterns of nature. Add a cluster of stones as a focal point. Position a vertical or horizontal log in the garden. Try to include water. A small drip emitter flowing into a shallow basin, such as a pot saucer, provides enough water to interest birds and butterflies.

Use materials found in your region. A decaying saguaro cactus is appropriate in the Southwest, but not the Northeast.

Group stones the same way you would group plants or a cluster of shrubs. Except in special cases, use stones in clusters of three or five (even numbers in the landscape look monotonous or too formally balanced) and offset them in an interesting way. Set a stone as though gravity had governed its fall. Stones rarely stand on end in nature. They are usually partially buried, so follow nature's way in the garden and dig a hole to nestle the stone into the earth. Try to use weathered stones. When set, they should look as if they had been there for centuries.

Both vertical and horizontal logs are interesting and provide shelter and food for wildlife. Squirrels will nest in a vertical log with a cavity, and woodpeckers will explore for grubs and other insects. A horizontal log makes an attractive place to sit. It can also serve as a low retaining wall supporting a grade change.

Dry-laid stone walls add character to grade changes in a garden. A short wall tucked into a slope or hillside can create a nook or sitting area under a clump of trees. A stone wall serves as a home for creatures such as newts, salamanders, and toads.

If you can't find logs, and stones are too heavy for you to lift, you can build a retaining wall with old railroad ties or simple planks. If you have to use new lumber, age it by painting it with a slurry of mason's lime.

Leave the slurry on for a couple of hours, then rinse it off. This will change the color of the wood and make it look aged.

A boulder placed flat on the ground, set slightly into the soil, looks like it has been there for centuries. This one suggests solidity and permanence.

Lady fern and wildflowers are massed together creating a thick groundcover in this meadow glen. Even just a few species repeated throughout the landscape create luxurious texture and color.

A waterfall, rock wall, and extensive plantings bring natural beauty to a tamed slope.

Years ago this meadow was a pond. Gradually it filled in and became a wet meadow; now trees are becoming established. This natural sequence of plant communities is called succession.

Among the growing regions of North America is the Eastern Deciduous Forest, a large area covering much of the eastern half of the continent.

THE REGIONS AND PLANTS OF NORTH AMERICA

Plant communities develop in response to the climate of their region. The climates of North America (see map on page 17) vary from hot and wet, to cool and dry, to cool and wet.

Learn what is natural in your region; then landscape accordingly. In regions with plentiful rainfall, forests are natural. When a clearing occurs in a forest, nature regenerates through succession. First a mixed meadow fills in the open space. The meadow eventually becomes a woodland. In time, this is replaced by the slower growing, larger trees. The whole process of regenerating the forest may take a century.

A large part of the North American continent is in climate zones that support forests. These include the Eastern Deciduous Forests, the Southern Forests and Coastal Plain along the Atlantic and the Gulf of Mexico, and the Western Mountains and Pacific Northwest. The common factor in these regions is ample rainfall occurring more or less evenly throughout the year. In another major region, the Central Prairies and Plains, the climax community is a combination of grasses and various annual and perennial plants. The Cold and Warm Western Deserts form another region. California Woodland and Brushland, the smallest region, is in a class by itself.

Within the major regions, climates are moderated by elevation or proximity to a large body of water. Even within your yard, the climate (called a microclimate) on the north side of your house is different from that on the south side. For more detailed information about your area, talk to a local horticulturist, a landscape architect, or your retail nursery, and visit your local library or bookstore for books and pamphlets about native plants.

The end of succession in nature is a climax community. This Douglas fir forest on Washington's Olympic Peninsula is an example.

PLANTS FOR NATURAL GARDENS

What does my land want to be? This is the first question to ask yourself as you embark upon the adventure of landscaping with nature.

Consider any plant that will thrive in your garden. Some plants from other parts of the world are as well-adapted here as any native. For instance, dandelions were brought to North America by European settlers but have now naturalized. Lilacs are not native to North America, but now act like they belong.

Sometimes this naturalizing process causes an imbalance in the native community. If there are no natural enemies, introduced species can multiply rapidly and crowd out native plants. Imported plants that grow too well, to the detriment of existing plants, are called invasive plants, and gardeners should avoid them. For more about invasive plants, see pages 78–79.

Because you live in a specific region, such as southwestern desert or eastern forest, doesn't mean you're doomed to an exclusive desert or woodland environment. Most landscapes are a mix. Instead the idea is to work with what you have and in the process reap the benefits of more birds, more butterflies, and more wildlife.

Subtle changes in the food chain cause shifts throughout the interconnected community of plants, animals, birds, and insects. In suburban areas where native plant communities have been replaced by introduced species, the number of bird species often decreases even though the total number of birds may increase.

For example, the native shrubs of California, such as those of the manzanita family, California lilac (*Ceanothus*), flannel bush, sumac, and California sage (*Artemisia*), and a nearly ubiquitous annual, California poppy, can thrive in other areas with moderate temperatures, dry summers, and ample winter rain.

Exotic species adapted to the same conditions can mix harmoniously with these native plants. Examples include plants from Australia and the Mediterranean area, both of which also have mild, wet winters and hot, dry summers. Many of the Australian eucalyptus thrive in California,

Some nonnative plants, such as this old garden rose in an abandoned cemetery, survive like native plants— without a gardener's care or attention.

This shrub garden in California relies on several drought-resistant plants, such as blue California lilac (Ceanothus), and rock rose (Cistus).

as do bottlebrush (*Callistemon*) and acacia. Sage (*Salvia*), bear's breeches (*Acanthus*), and valerian (*Valeriana officinalis*), all native to the hills of Italy and Greece, grow well in California gardens.

The Pacific Northwest has a climate much like that in England. For this reason, the advice found in some of the excellent British gardening books can be followed successfully for this region. The Northeast and Midwest have climates similar to Central Europe. Early settlers of these areas were able to bring many native plants with them. Such species have become so common in gardens in these areas that they are accepted as native.

Aesthetics plays a role in your natural garden too. Interesting contrasts and dramatic opposing forms can be used to enhance your garden. But nature rarely displays disharmony. Although many plants will grow and even naturalize in temperate zones, mixing plants from the far corners of the world with natives in your natural garden may not always look right. Compare the shapes, colors, and textures of your plants and decide if they form a visually harmonious combination.

This Washington, D.C., garden shows how plant choice and placement can suggest a native planting. Only the green yucca (center) is native. The grass behind it is reed grass (Calamagrostis epigejos) a noninvasive European native.

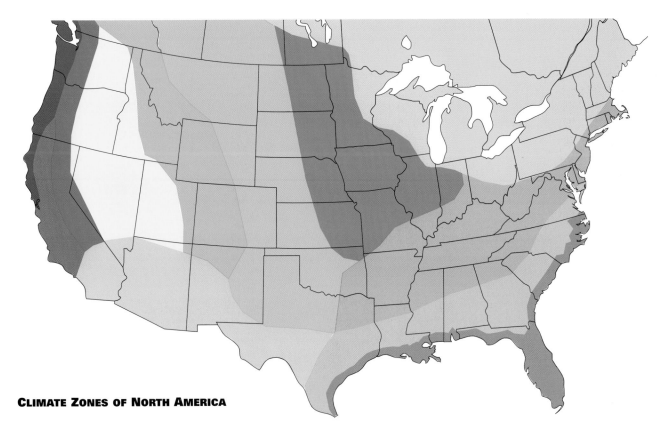

CLIMATE ZONES OF NORTH AMERICA

Western Mountains and Pacific Northwest
- Pacific Forests
- Sierra-Cascades
- Rocky Mountains

California Brushland and Woodland
- California Brushland and Woodland

Western Deserts
- Cold Deserts
- Warm Deserts

Central Prairies and Plains
- Short Grass Prairies
- Tall Grass Prairies

Eastern Deciduous Forests
- Northern Forests
- Central Forests

Southern Forests
- Inland Forests
- Coastal Plains

THE NATURAL REGIONS OF NORTH AMERICA

EASTERN DECIDUOUS FORESTS

This large region extends from the southern portion of eastern Canada, west to Minnesota, and south to eastern Texas and northern Georgia. It encompasses the northeastern United States and most of the Great Lakes. The northern part is generally cold with sometimes severe winters. The region receives an annual precipitation of 20 to 40 inches evenly spread throughout the year, which creates a humid climate that supports a wide mix of plants.

Glacial action during the last Ice Age shaped and molded the area. In addition to sculpting the Great Lakes, it created the thousands of lakes and wetlands in the region. Rising above the lakes and bogs are low, hilly areas called a moraine, great piles of stone, gravel, and sand that are another product of the glaciers. Although the region's forests are predominantly deciduous and mixed, coniferous trees are also common.

The coniferous trees of this region are red cedar, pine, hemlock, some larch, and spruce. Deciduous trees include maple, paper birch, beech, oak, walnut, ash, and basswood (also known as American linden). Undergrowth includes hazelnut, dogwood, serviceberry, redbud, some shrubby maple, bearberry, and many wildflowers. Hardy rhododendrons are common. Lush ferns, Dutchman's breeches, trout lily, and windflower (*Anemone*) sprout in spring, when sunlight can penetrate through the leafless canopy.

Because of the reliable moisture, many other hardy plants adapt easily to this region and naturalize so they seem to be part of the native community. The usually rich soils and adequate moisture make this area ideal for agriculture, and many of the heavily forested areas have been cleared for farming or development.

Eastern Deciduous Forests (below) have ample rain through a long growing season and cold winters.

Pickleweed and tropical sage grow in this marsh on the outer coastal plain of Florida.

SOUTHERN FORESTS

The Southern Forests are broken into two distinct sections. The Coastal Plain is one and extends from the Gulf Coast, along the Mississippi Delta, across northern Florida, and north along

This restored tall-grass prairie in Whitnall Park, Wisconsin, includes yellow Ratibida, purple Liatris, purple coneflower (Echinacea) and white Queen-Anne's-lace, a wildflower from Europe.

the Atlantic. Although this region is a relatively narrow strip along the coast, conditions vary considerably, and many plant populations merge into a number of distinct communities. The region supports a wealth of native plants, many of which have adapted in other parts of North America. With its ample moisture and humid climate, this region has a year-round gardening season.

Much of the immediate coast is clear sand beach with no vegetation merging into dunes with a rich variety of grasses and other salt-tolerant species. Throughout the lowlands of this region are marshes and bogs, broad rich river deltas, and wetlands with the water table near the surface.

The forests of bald cypress and gum (*Nyssa*) found in the lower wetlands give way to communities of magnolia, live oak, and Carolina laurel cherry (*Prunus caroliniana*) on the slightly higher lands and river deltas. From southern Virginia to southeastern Texas, much of the predominant forest is long-leaf pine, a large tree with 12- to 18-inch needles. It grows on grassy plains along with prairielike perennials that are fire tolerant.

The second section of the southern forests is the inland regions—the rolling foothills east of the Appalachians and central Gulf Coast states, where the land slopes gently toward the sea. Here the climate is mild and heavy rain occurs throughout the year. In contrast to other forest regions, much of the soil in this one is depleted of nutrients; they leach out because the soil is often warm when it rains.

This open forest area is dominated by loblolly and shortleaf pines. Grasses are the primary understory. Many fires occur in the pine-and-grass environments, but the forest is extremely fire tolerant and recovers quickly.

The lowlands near the coast are often boggy. Here the forest changes to bald cypress and gum. On some of the higher land above the bogs, stands of hickory and oak shelter an understory of evergreen broad-leaved shrubs, including viburnum, blueberry, and dogwood.

CENTRAL PRAIRIES AND PLAINS

Grasslands once occupied a great swath through the Central Prairies and Plains of North America. In these regions— where moisture from rain and snow is too meager to sustain trees, or periodic fires burn tree and shrub seedlings— grasses predominate. Grasslands still cover large areas, but where soils were fertile the prairies and plains have been tilled for agricultural purposes. Perennials thrive in grasslands too, and when they bloom they seem more prolific than they really are. Trees and shrubs cluster in groves along streams and in low, moist areas.

Grassland can be divided into the tall-grass prairies and the short-grass plains. Tall-grass prairies, which thrive in regions of heavy rainfall, extend from Alberta in the north through Nebraska, Iowa, Kansas, Missouri, Illinois, and Indiana. The dominant grasses are big bluestem (*Andropogon gerardii*), little bluestem (*Schizachyrium scoparium*), northern dropseed (*Sporobolus heterolepis*), and Indiangrass (*Sorghastrum nutans*). Native tall-grass prairies were so high that children could become lost in them, and even adults had trouble seeing over the tops of the grasses.

Short-grass plains extend from the Rocky Mountains to the northeast corner of Colorado and the northwest corner of Texas, where the climate is dry. Buffalograss (*Buchloe dactyloides*), blue gramagrass (*Bouteloua gracilis*), and needle-and-thread grass (*Stipa comata*) are the predominant species here.

Many low-growing annuals and tall perennials native to the prairies and plains that thrive in the arid garden are discussed in more detail in the chapter beginning on page 26.

Little bluestem, like other prairie grasses, changes dramatically with the seasons.

Rocky Mountain bee plant brightens a short-grass plain in eastern Colorado.

THE NATURAL REGIONS OF NORTH AMERICA
continued

Rocky Mountain forests offer a variety of scenery and ecosystems because of the rugged terrain and range of elevations. At high elevations and on steep slopes, only rugged alpine plants grow.

WESTERN MOUNTAINS AND PACIFIC NORTHWEST

Although the Rocky Mountain Forest, the Sierras, the Cascade Forest, and the Pacific Forest are different regions, their many similarities allow them to be categorized into one large section. They are all precipitous mountain regions with cascading rivers and wide variations caused by extremes in elevation, precipitation, and available light. Some of the deep valleys between the mountains receive only a few hours of sunshine each day.

All of these areas boast high alpine meadows with short growing seasons above the timberline, a band of stunted and windswept coniferous trees at the higher elevations just below the meadows, and mixed pines blending into a thick forest of Douglas fir at somewhat lower elevations.

At the higher elevations of the Rocky Mountains is a mix of Engelmann spruce and limber pine. At lower levels ponderosa pine and quaking aspen mix with Douglas fir.

All parts of nature are dependent on one another. Here, a fallen tree in a redwood forest provides support and nutrients for sword ferns, which will provide nutrients for other plants when they die.

A few shrubs, grasses, and perennials fill in the clearings. Depending on elevation and moisture conditions, the shrubs might include elderberry, Oregon grape, bearberry, California lilac, sumac, serviceberry, hazelnut, juniper, and dogwood. Some common perennials in these mountain habitats are columbine, penstemon, coral bells, Indian paintbrush (*Castilleja indivisa*), and lupine. Many of these trees, shrubs, and perennials adapt well in the garden and are available at local nurseries.

The subalpine section of these mountains includes red fir, lodgepole pine, and mountain hemlock. Below that, Jeffrey pine, incense cedar, and sugar pine mix with Douglas fir. Giant redwoods can be found in isolated groves in the Sierras. In the lower elevations are ponderosa pine and Jeffrey pine with a grass understory.

The Pacific Forest area has extreme variations in its climates. Whereas the southern section is dry, with only about 20 inches of rainfall each year, the Olympic Peninsula might receive as much as 300 inches of rain a year; it supports a rain forest. Most of the region's climate is mild and even, but on the higher western slopes of the Cascade mountains, wind-driven storms and an occasional incursion of arctic air can cause severe weather and temperature conditions.

Much of this region has dense forests of Douglas fir, western red cedar, hemlock, and Sitka spruce. In coastal northern California the coast redwood is the dominant tree.

The most diverse forests in this temperate zone are on the Olympic Peninsula in northern Washington and on the west coast of Vancouver Island, where there is a rain forest. The copious water supply encourages a dense understory of rhododendrons, vine maple, currants, ferns, and mosses, as well as a profusion of perennials.

WESTERN DESERTS

Deserts in North America are divided into cold desert and warm desert.

The cold desert extends from Nevada in the south to Idaho and Washington state in the north. It is generally high country with cold winters. A finger of this desert extends up the Okanagan Valley into British Columbia, where you can find cactus growing. These areas are protected from rainfall by surrounding mountains; their precipitation levels are less than 20 inches a year. Summer days are hot and dry, but frost can occur in any month of the year, especially at the higher elevations. Winters are moderately to severely cold.

Typical cold-desert plants include sagebrush (*Artemisia arbuscula*), saltbush, chamise (*Ademostoma fasciculatum*), desert olive, and yucca. A few species of cacti are native to these deserts as well. In the southern areas some stands of piñon pine manage in better soils. In the northern section, there are pockets of ponderosa pine along the desert perimeter. Where rainfall is greatest, some perennial grasses also thrive. After occasional summer rains, short-lived annuals sprout from seed and bloom almost immediately.

Arid climates do not support a forest. Instead, the climax plant community is desert, short-grass prairie, brushland, or a woodland of widely separated small trees.

In this Cold Desert of eastern Oregon, the sagebrush plants grow far apart, optimizing limited water.

THE NATURAL REGIONS OF NORTH AMERICA
continued

The warm desert (above) *is home to the stately saguaro cactus.*

In warm deserts, ocotillo (Fouquieria splendens) is a favorite of the black-chinned hummingbird.

The Warm Deserts include the Mojave predominantly in California, the Sonoran of California, Arizona, and northern Mexico, and the Chihuahuan of Arizona, southern New Mexico, and Texas. These deserts are arid. Some areas can be without rainfall for as long as two years.

The hallmark of desert landscapes is the occasional brilliant display of wildflowers after spring rains. The Mojave is known for its spectacular Joshua trees; brittlebush, creosote bush, and allscale are common shrubs. Las Vegas is the best-known city in this region.

The Sonoran desert has the mildest winters of these desert regions. Winter nighttime temperatures rarely drop below 0° F. Rainfall varies from 2 to 12 inches annually. In areas with the most moisture, many species of cacti flourish. Shrubs of this region are ocotillo and brittlebush. Trees include desert willow, mesquite, ironwood, and paloverde.

The Chihuahuan desert is cold. Winter temperatures can drop as low as –15° F, and summer heat can reach 120° F. Precipitation is a little greater than in the Sonoran and comes in the form of winter snow and summer downpours. Flash floods are common. Cacti are plentiful; generally, smaller types grow here. Among the many trees and shrubs native to this area are creosotebush, desert willow, honey mesquite, ocotillo, sumac, and Texas sage (*Leucophyllum frutescens*). Wildflowers, too, are plentiful, including blackfoot daisy, penstemon, morning glory, and desert zinnia (*Zinnia grandiflora*). Grasses include Indian rice grass (*Oryzopsis hymenoides*) and sand love grass (*Eragrostis trichodes*), which adapt well in a natural garden.

WOODLAND AND BRUSHLAND

At the desert edges, where rainfall is less than 20 inches annually but enough to support tree and shrub cover, woodlands or shrublands occur, particularly where the rainfall is seasonal. A woodland is a forest with only 30 to 70 percent cover and lots of open shrub and meadow area. The light that filters through the thin forest cover fosters the growth of an active understory.

The typical woodland at desert edges is the Piñon-Juniper Woodland, found on the Colorado Plateau of Arizona, New Mexico, southern Utah, and Colorado. The dominant trees are piñon pine and juniper. Few of these small trees exceed 25 to 30 feet in height. They are widely spaced and typically have an understory of serviceberry, some manzanita, cliffrose, and some grasses. Piñon pine, serviceberry, and some types of manzanita are adaptable to the arid garden.

Chaparral is common in California from sea level to 8,000 feet. It is a plant community of evergreen shrubs with tough, leathery leaves. Arizona also supports a few areas of chaparral. Summers in these regions are hot and dry, and winter rain fall varies from 12 to 40 inches annually. Plants must tolerate drought but also survive occasional heavy rainfall. The woodland trees associated with these areas are evergreen oaks (*Quercus*) and madrone (*Arbutus menziesii*). The understory plants are manzanita (*Arctostaphylos*), California lilac (*Ceanothus*), and toyon (*Heteromeles arbutifolia*). Near streams in these areas, a woodland of California sycamore (*Platanus racemosa*), alder (*Alnus spp.*), and cottonwood (*Populus fremontii*) develops.

Brilliant blue native lupine and Santa Barbara ceanothus (Ceanothus impressus) cover and protect a hillside.

Manzanita is typical of the dense brush of California's chaparral. Mostly evergreen, with small, tough leaves, chaparral plants grow in spring and fall, when weather is warm and the soil moist.

YOUR REGION IS KEY

A surprising number of flowering plants (below) thrive and bloom in the shade of a woodland garden. For the greatest variety and fullest bloom, thin the trees so that the shade is not too heavy.

Purple spikes of Liatris (above) accent a patch of wildflowers that also includes white Queen Anne's lace, feverfew (small white daisies), and yellow Ratibida.

Once you know about the natural landscape where you live, you can add features of it that you like and that work in your own garden. Whether prairie or woodland, arid or wet, there are exciting native plants—and noninvasive exotic plants—you can use.

If you live in a region with ample moisture, you can create a meadow by simply not mowing. Existing lawn grasses will get shaggy. Gradually other plants will introduce themselves as natural succession begins to create a woodland on its way to becoming a climax forest.

Combined shrub and tree woodlands form the characteristic edge between meadows and forests. These woodlands host a rich diversity of plant species, colors, and textures. Regular thinning of the tree canopy to ensure dappled rather than dense shade affords you the best selection of plants for your yard.

Encourage perennials and groundcovers to drift among the shrubs and into the tree background, adding color and texture to the overall picture.

In an arid climate converting your existing lawn into a meadow by not watering will likely result in an invasion of hardy weeds.

Instead, kill the lawn grass and plant a combination of hardy shrubs and trees and adapted wildflowers.

Growing a prairie will require experimentation and some commitment to maintenance until a balanced community of plants becomes established in your yard. If you live in a very dry region, plan on irrigating for at least one season.

A low spot in your garden can simulate a natural pond or bog and provide a sanctuary for a wide variety of plants and animals. Even in arid climates a pond will attract and support frogs, newts, and other amphibians that could not survive without water.

In some regions a fairly large pond can be sustained simply by diverting water from the roof of the house into a depression in the ground. This also helps to prevent overloading the local storm sewer.

There's more about each of these basic types of gardens in the next chapters.

Ponds (above) add life and interest to gardens. They provide a setting for a variety of water-loving plants and animals as well as fish.

As this tadpole (right) completes its change into a frog, it absorbs its gills and becomes an air breather.

A spring bloom of bitterbrush (Encina) steals the show in this desert garden. Note that without water, natural-looking bare spaces sprout few weeds.

This prairie garden is lit up with perennials, including purple coneflower (rear) and Liatris (front).

NATURAL GARDENS IN ARID REGIONS

Much of North America west of the 100th meridian (from western Manitoba and the central Dakotas south through Texas) is arid, meaning it receives less than 25 inches of precipitation a year. These regions are dry and hot in the summer but may have very cold winters. Among the arid plant communities are the Central Prairies and Plains, the Piñon-Juniper Woodland, the California Woodland and Brushland, and the Deserts, the most arid receiving less than 10 inches of rain annually.

Three types of natural landscape adapt themselves to gardens in arid regions: prairies, shrublands and woodlands, and true deserts. Your arid garden will probably reflect the character of one or more of these types. This section describes the kinds of plants to use generally, and then specifically, in lists. Select the type of garden that is most natural to your area or best fits into your yard. You can mix the types, although one of them will probably be dominant.

LOCATION, LOCATION, LOCATION

Arid gardens thrive in full sun, although the dappled shade cast by small, lightly branched trees will increase the number of plants you can grow. Most arid-region plants prefer lean, sandy or gravelly loam with good drainage.

By carefully siting your garden, you can grow plants that are normally too tender for your climate. For example, plants next to the house will be warmed by the heat lost through the building's outer walls; plants on the south side of the house or a fence or other structure will be warmed by reflected sunlight.

Another way to help marginal plants survive in a cold climate is to mulch. Before the first hard freeze in fall, place a few inches of organic or inorganic mulch over the root area of each plant. Remove organic mulches after the spring thaw in cold winter regions.

Home gardeners can adapt the look of a dry prairie garden by using combinations like this one, featuring black-eyed Susans, purplish 'Autumn Joy' sedum, and ornamental grasses.

PLANTS OF ARID REGIONS

Many trees, shrubs, and other plants either are native to arid regions or will adapt to your garden if the temperature range isn't too different from their native lands. Some of the best plants for arid gardens are listed on these pages.

SHRUBS: Although shrubs for natural arid gardens come in a wide range of sizes, flower and foliage color, and texture, shrubs native to dry climates exhibit some common traits. Leaves are frequently leathery, small, and sparse or covered with hairs, all of which inhibit moisture loss.

A French formal landscape with sheared hedges and rigid symmetry beautifully complements California's Napa Valley.

Most drought-resistant plants prefer full sun or dappled shade. Most sun-loving plants will tolerate some shade with no ill effects if they receive at least six hours of full sun a day. Shrubs that prefer shade should be protected from the hot afternoon sun.

The accompanying lists on pages 35–37 include shrubs native to North America as well ones that are not native, but grow as if they were. Many will adapt to all arid regions. Most of them prefer well-drained soil.

GRASSES: Dramatic and graceful, grasses are excellent additions to the arid garden. Even a gentle breeze will cause them to sway delightfully, adding interest to a quiet landscape. Grasses that have turned brown in late summer can be even more beautiful than when fully green in early spring.

Drought-resistant prairie grasses range in height from a few inches to 8 feet. In a large garden, group together the tallest grasses in the background. Most small and medium grasses are good additions to perennial or shrub borders.

Buffalograss (*Buchloe dactyloides*) is an excellent lawn grass in arid regions. It turns a bronzy purple at the first frost, then turns brown through the winter and early spring. Typically growing only 6 to 8 inches high, it is an effective groundcover with or without mowing. For a textured lawn, mow it two or three times a year to keep it thick and controlled. An effective transition from lawn areas to the arid tree and shrub background can be created by using a low-growing grass such as northern dropseed (*Sporobolus heterolepsis*) or blue gramagrass (*Bouteloua gracilis*).

WILDFLOWERS AND PERENNIALS: Not only are flowering plants a delight to the eye, but they are also vitally important to wildlife. Birds, for instance, depend on berries and dry-seeded fruits as food sources.

Grow some wildflowers and perennials from seed;

Purple coneflower (Echinacea purpurea) and orange butterfly weed (Asclepias tuberosa) are superb nectar flowers for butterflies. Pearly everlasting (Anaphalis margaritacea) is a favorite caterpillar host plant for the American Lady butterfly.

When gardening in a desert climate, choose plants that are native to the area. Native prickly pear cactus, for example, stands up to heat and drought and produces spectacular springtime flowers.

The southwest has extreme heat and aridity, but with irrigation its list of landscape trees is long. Today, however, the emphasis is on drought-tolerant species and desert natives to pair with the hot, dry landscape.

others are best raised from corms, bulbs, rootstocks or plants.

Plant wildflower seeds in fall. The winter rain or snow cover will germinate them. Then they will wait until warm spring weather to grow. Wildflower seeds are usually tiny and expensive per ounce, but a small quantity will plant a large area. Mix the seed with sharp, dry sand before broadcasting; it is much easier to handle a small quantity of seed that way.

GROUNDCOVERS: These plants may be used as a lawn substitute, as low plants tucked into rock gardens or dry-laid stone walls, as fillers between stepping-stones, or simply to cover the ground between shrubs or under trees. When used as a lawn substitute, a well-established groundcover will inhibit the growth of weeds.

SUCCULENTS AND CACTI: These desert plants are very drought-resistant and trouble-free once they are established. They all need full sun. Almost all cacti demand lean and well-drained soil. Many will bloom dramatically after spring and summer rains. Most will overwinter in Zone 5 (see page 92).

Once desert natives are established, they rarely need fertilizing or watering. Most however, appreciate some soil preparation when originally planted. For planting backfill, mix a small amount of local compost into rock-free soil excavated from the planting hole. Follow planting by mulching with coarse organic material such as composted bark or with an inch or two of crushed stone or washed gravel to conserve moisture.

Planting cacti and succulents amid boulders and stones complements the rugged character of these plants. In nature, cacti grow far apart, so allow room between plants.

SOIL PROBLEMS IN ARID REGIONS

Installing a natural garden in arid regions begins below the ground level. Some drought-resistant plants are shallow rooted; their root system is spread over a large area to capture moisture when it comes. Soil for these plants needs to be loose and friable. Slope the surface of the soil to avoid standing water. To check for drainage, dig some test holes about 2 feet deep and fill them with water. When the water has drained away, fill the hole again. The water level should drop at least 6 inches in 24 hours.

In the West, where rainfall is low, unique soil conditions may evolve. Soils high in sodium salts are called sodic soils. Though rare, they drain very poorly and often have a top layer impervious to water. Correct this condition by incorporating gypsum into the soil followed by very heavy watering. The calcium in the gypsum will replace the sodium and improve the soil's structure. Before treating this condition, test the soil to confirm the presence of high sodium.

Another soil condition is common in southwestern deserts. Called *caliche*, it is a layer of cementlike lime (calcium carbonate). It makes a hard layer of soil that roots and water cannot penetrate. Also, its high pH restricts the ability of most plants to absorb some nutrients.

Ideally, dig completely through the caliche layer before planting. If that's not practical, dig a narrow drainage hole at the bottom of the planting hole through the caliche. This will provide the necessary water drainage.

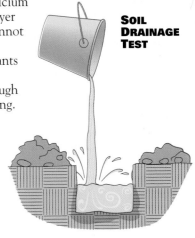

SOIL DRAINAGE TEST

ARID WOODLANDS

In California, grasses and purple-flowered **Brodiaea** *under live oaks are lush in spring. They'll dry and turn golden by June.*

Beardlip penstemon (Penstemon barbatus) in a southwestern garden.

California lilac (Ceanothus) is a native plant that grows well in California.

A woodland is an open forest, an environment still dominated by trees, but where the trees provide only 30 to 70 percent cover.

These shrubby or wooded plant communities grow in many of the same regions as prairies and share some of the same grasses, annuals, and perennials. When prairies are overgrazed and the grasses are thinned out, other vegetation can then grow, and shrublands and woodlands may gradually dominate.

Unlike prairie grasses, which grow deep into the soil to find water during the dry season, shrubby and wooded plants in arid regions often have shallow, spreading root systems and small, leathery leaves that inhibit moisture loss. The plants adapt to drought by conserving water and then drinking quickly at each rain with their extensive roots. In some woodlands, small pines, such as piñon pine, are the dominant tree. Some arid woodlands are sparse; the plants are widely spaced and bare earth is exposed.

The rugged character of arid shrublands and woodlands is easy to duplicate in your garden. Once established, a shrubland garden is easy to maintain; it requires little water, almost no fertilizer, and only a little pruning.

Woodland trees are not usually the taller species of forested regions but are often smaller trees, some almost shrublike in size. Because a woodland is an open community with ample light, it usually has many shrubs, annuals and perennials, and grasses in the understory. Major woodlands of North America are the Piñon-Juniper Woodland of the American Southwest and the Great Basin (the area between the Sierra Nevada and the Rockies), and the Evergreen-Oak Woodland of the California chaparral.

Shrublands also occur in these climatic conditions of reduced and seasonal rainfall and are usually dense growths of broad-leaved evergreen shrubs or small, shrublike trees, both with hard, leathery leaves and other adaptations to water stress. Chaparral is an evergreen shrubland in much of southern and central California and in scattered areas of the Southwest.

PIÑON-JUNIPER WOODLAND: On the deeply cut Colorado Plateau of Arizona, New Mexico, southern Utah, and Colorado grows an open woodland of piñon pine and several species of juniper. Soils are poor and stony. The woodland trees are small—rarely taller than 30 feet—and scattered. Between the trees grow shrubs of serviceberry, cliffrose, and other species, and a sparse groundcover of short grasses. Because of its elevation (5,000 to 7,000 feet), the Colorado Plateau's climate varies from other areas of the Southwest: Winters are cold and summers are hot days with cool nights. Temperatures are lower at higher elevations. Rainfall is about 20 inches a year, although local dry areas may only receive 10 inches, and rain falls in both summer and winter. Areas that are drier or lower in elevation can generally support only a sparse grassland.

Piñon-Juniper Woodland also marks the highest-elevation life zone of the Great Basin, growing on the rocky ridges and low mountains above the sagebrush-clad basins.

Piñon-Juniper Woodland is dominated by species of pine and juniper that, though similar, change somewhat from state to state. Consult your local nursery to see which species are native to your area. Piñons and junipers should be widely spaced so that the shrubs and small plants that grow among them receive the sunlight they need. All the plants of the appropriate grassland lists can be grown in the sunniest spots of a piñon-juniper planting.

PLANTS OF WESTERN WOODLANDS

Latin Name	Common Names	Description
PIÑON-JUNIPER WOODLAND		
Trees		
Acer glabrum	Rocky Mountain maple	Scarlet fall color; shrub or small tree
Juniperus species	Juniper	Plants fragrant, becoming gnarled; silvery berries
Pinus cembroides and P. monophylla	Piñon pines	Cones produce edible nuts
Shrubs		
Artemisia tridentata	Big sagebrush	Soft, gray foliage
Cercocarpus species	Mountain mahogany	Shrub or low tree; subtle
Chrysothamnus nauseosus	Rabbitbrush	Whitish; showy yellow flowers
Opuntia imbricata	Cane cactus	Red flowers and yellow fruit
Quercus gambeli	Gambel's oak	White oak; gold fall color
Shepherdia argentea	Buffalo berry	To 18 feet; thorny; edible fruit
Annuals and Perennials		
Castilleja integra	Indian paintbrush	Showy red bracts resembling flowers at branch tips
Lesquerella arizonica	Bladderpod	Yellow flowers
Liatris punctata	Blazing star	Purple; fall bloomer
Penstemon barbatus	Beardlip	Attracts hummingbirds
Zinnia grandiflora	Wild zinnia	Small yellow daisy; little resemblance to garden zinnia
CHAPARRAL AND OAK WOODLAND		
Trees		
Acer macrophyllum	Bigleaf maple	Fast-growing; to 100 feet
Arbutus menziesii	Madrone	Red bark and berries
Pinus coulteri	Coulter pine	Large dark blue-green cones
Prunus ilicifolia	Holly-leaved cherry	Small evergreen tree; large shrub
Prunus lyonii	Catalina cherry	Evergreen; dark green narrowly ovate leaves
Quercus agrifolia	Coast live oak	Evergreen; gnarled
Quercus lobata	Valley oak	Large; deciduous
Umbellularia californica	California laurel	Leaves can be substituted for bay leaves in cooking
Shrubs		
Arctostaphylos species	Manzanita	Many species in cultivation
Carpenteria californica	Carpenteria	Needs some shade; showy white flowers
Ceanothus species	California lilac	Showy groundcovers and shrubs
Dendromecon rigida harfordii	Island bush poppy	Flowers yellow; needs sandy soil
Eriogonum giganteum	St.-Catherine's-lace	Used in dried flower arrangements
Fremontodendron californicum	Flannel bush	Showy yellow flowers; requires well-drained soil
Heteromeles arbutifolia	Toyon	Evergreen; red berries are important winter bird food
Mimulus aurantiacus	Monkeyflower	Yellow flowers throughout the year
Rhamnus californica	Coffeeberry	To 6 feet; evergreen; understory species
Ribes viburnifolium	Catalina currant	Adaptable as groundcover; in shade under oaks
Salvia clevelandii	Cleveland sage	Leaves can be substituted for culinary sage
Annuals and Perennials		
Clarkia biloba	Clarkia	Notched petals; needs sun
Dodecatheon sp.	Shooting star	Flowers of white, magenta, lavender, or purple
Epilobium canum ssp. canum	California fuchsia	Red flowers in late summer and fall
Iris douglasiana	Wild iris	Flowers from shades of purple to cream or white
Romneya coulteri	Matilija poppy	Very large and showy; grows in canyons in nature but adapts well to cultivation

SHORT-GRASS PLAINS

Red Indian paintbrush and bluebonnets are brilliant and easy-to-grow wildflowers of the short-grass plains.

Native purple, pink, and white penstemons bloom with all the color and charm of any exotic flower.

Kansas gayfeather (Liatris pycnostachya) graced by an eastern tiger swallowtail.

With lower rainfall and heavier, less fertile soils, tall-grass prairie gradually diminishes toward the west, blending into the short-grass plains of Alberta, the western Dakotas, Montana, Wyoming, Colorado, and the Texas Panhandle. The elevation of this Great Plains region gradually rises from 2,500 feet in the east to 5,000 feet at the western edge, where it meets the Rocky Mountains. The land surface is broken in some regions by canyons, rugged buttes, and tumbled badlands.

In this semiarid region, the high sod-forming grasses predominant in the tall-grass prairie give way to shorter grasses, many of which are bunchgrasses. These do not provide 100 percent cover, and they alternate with patches of bare ground.

Many annuals and perennials flower in spring and summer, including sunflower, evening primrose, coneflower, and Indian paintbrush. Trees and shrubs are scattered; isolated individuals of bur oak and cottonwood occupy sheltered or moist habitats, and mesquite and cactus are common in some areas, especially in Colorado and Wyoming.

Short-grass plains are found in several other regions of the West. Bordering the warm southwestern deserts in Arizona and New Mexico is an arid grassland of gramagrass and other species, dotted with desert shrubs and cacti in open stands. An extensive grassland once covered the Central Valley of California; this may have been mostly species of needlegrass but is now almost completely agricultural fields and grasslands of imported annual grasses. The Palouse region of eastern Washington and Oregon once supported extensive grasslands of bluebunch wheatgrass, fescue, and bluegrass, intermingled in some areas with Great Basin sagebrush and the forest trees of the nearby mountains. This area also is now used mostly for agriculture.

PLANTS OF CENTRAL AND SOUTHERN PRAIRIES AND PLAINS

Latin Name	Common Name	Description
SHRUBS		
Bumelia lanuginosa	False buckthorn	Small shrub with fragrant flowers
Dalea formosa and D. frutescens	Indigo bush	Small-leaved shrubs with bicolored purple and rose flowers
Hesperaloe parviflora	Real yucca	Blooms spring to midsummer in dry soils
Parkinsonia aculeata	Jerusalem thorn	Shrub or small tree to 40 feet; showy yellow flowers
Prosopis glandulosa	Honey mesquite	Multitrunked shrub or small tree with drooping branches
Quercus macrocarpa	Bur oak	Can become large tree
Rhus aromatica	Fragrant sumac	Aromatic leaves; yellow flowers in spike clusters
Sophora secundiflora	Mescal bean	Scarlet beans are quite poisonous
Ungnadia speciosa	Spanish buckeye	Shrub or small tree with large flowers; seeds may be poisonous
Yucca glauca	Great Plains yucca	Stemless rosettes of basal leaves with 2- to 4-foot spikes of creamy white flowers in midsummer
ANNUALS AND PERENNIALS		
Allium stellatum	Wild onion	Pink flowers
Asclepias tuberosa	Butterfly weed	Showy orange or yellow flowers
Asclepias viridifolia	Green milkweed	Subtle; to nearly 3 feet
Aster kumleinii	Aster	Purple with gold center
Astragalus species	Milk vetch	Many species; inquire locally for availability
Baptisia australis	Blue false indigo	Handsome flowers and form
Baptisia leucophaea	Cream baptisia	Very showy legume; inflated pods
Cucurbita foetidissima	Buffalo gourd	Vine; green and yellow striped fruit
Echinacea purpurea	Purple coneflower	Purple daisy with gold-brown center
Echinocereus baileyi	Hedgehog cactus	See piñon-juniper list for other species
Eustoma grandiflorum	Tulip gentian	Very showy purple flowers
Ipomopsis (Gilia) rubra	Standing cypress	6-foot scarlet spikes
Liatris punctata, L. pycnostachya, and L. squarrosa	Blazing star	Purple spikes in late summer and fall
Lupinus texensis	Texas bluebonnet	Texas state flower
Mentzelia decapetala	Queen-of-the-plains	Large cream flowers; requires good drainage
Monarda fistulosa	Wild bergamot	Lavender; ranges over much of North America
Oenothera missouriensis	Missouri primrose	Large, lemon yellow flowers; papery winged pods
Oenothera speciosa	Showy evening primrose	Flowers white, rarely pink
Palafoxia hookerana	Othake rosywings	Limited natural distribution in sandy soils; showy pink flowers
Penstemon species	Penstemon	Flowers white, rose, lavender, or purple, depending on species
Petalostemon multiflorus	Prairie clover	White
Petalostemon purpureum	Purple prairie clover	Purple; to 3 feet
Ratibida columnifera	Column coneflower	Maroon or yellow rays
Salvia pitcheri	Blue sage	Abundant bloomer
Solidago mollis	Goldenrod	Gray leaves; gold flowers
Sphaeralcea coccinea	Scarlet mallow	Showy flowers

DESERTS

In deserts, use native or native-like species, but planted more densely than they would naturally occur. The result is a colorful and interesting landscape, like the one shown here.

California fuchsia (Epilobium canum ssp. canum) lives up to its nickname of hummingbird flower.

In some parts of the western United States, precipitation is extremely low and irregular, temperatures are high, and strong drying winds are common. Such a climate severely limits plant growth. Widely spaced plants adapt in various ways to maximize the small amount of water that is available. The deserts of the United States are the cold desert of the Great Basin and the warm deserts of southeast California, Arizona, New Mexico, and west Texas.

COLD DESERTS: The region that includes Nevada, southern Oregon and Idaho, western Utah, and northwestern California is composed of numerous interior basins dissected by steep, parallel mountain ranges. Few streams drain to the coast. The region is at fairly high elevation (near 5,000 feet), and some of its mountains rise 2,000 feet above the basin floors. This is an area of little precipitation; rainfall amounts range from 5 to 20 inches annually, mostly in winter. Summers are hot, and winters moderately cold. Frost may occur any month of the year.

The major plant, growing in widely spaced, open stands, is big sagebrush. A number of other shrubs are dominant in moist areas, strongly alkaline soils, or soils with high salt concentrations, including rabbitbrush, shadscale, and saltbush. Few trees are present in the basins, although Piñon-Juniper Woodland grows at the higher elevations in the mountains. Many short-lived annual flowers germinate and bloom after spring and summer rains.

WARM DESERTS: This community includes several deserts in the southwest: the Mojave of Arizona, California, and Nevada; the Sonoran of predominently Arizona and northern Mexico, and the Chihuahuan mostly in southern New Mexico, west Texas, and Mexico. Although their climates are similar, there are some differences, and each area supports slightly different desert vegetation. Rainfall in all three areas is very low and irregular. It falls mainly as erratic winter rains in the Mojave Desert, winter and summer rains in the Sonoran Desert,

PLANTS OF COLD DESERTS

The following list covers shrubs and wildflowers of the basin floor and foothills. Mountain islands of higher elevations in the Great Basin support a piñon-juniper forest, with plants similar to higher elevation Rocky Mountain flora.

Latin Name	Common Name	Description
SHRUBS		
Artemisia tridentata	Big sagebrush	Gray; abundant
Chrysothamnus nauseosus	Rabbitbrush	Gray; showy yellow flower clusters in autumn
Cowania mexicana	Cliff rose	Dry slopes
Ephedra viridis	Mormon tea	Green "stick" plants
Fallugia paradoxa	Apache plume	White flowers; fluffy seed heads
Haplopappus acaulis	Haplopappus	Yellow daisies on shrubby mats
Holodiscus boursieri	Oceanspray	Dry rocky slopes
Peraphyllum ramosissimum	Shrub of rose family	Desert washes
Purshia tridentata	Bitterbrush	To 10 feet
Shepherdia argentea	Buffalo berry	Needs moisture
ANNUALS AND PERENNIALS		
Allium anceps	Wild onion	Rose flowers with purple midveins
Astragalus pterocarpus	Winged seed milk vetch	Flowers purple or white
Astragalus purshii	Pursh's milk vetch	Woolly pods
Baileya multiradiata	Desert marigold	Very showy
Balsamorhiza sagittata	Arrow-leaved balsamroot	Yellow daisies
Cymopterus globosus	Cymopterus	Ground-hugging herb in parsley family
Delphinium andersonii	Anderson's larkspur	Grows with sagebrush
Epilobium canum ssp. canum	California fuchsia	Showy scarlet flowers; attract hummingbirds
Erigeron species	Daisies	Flowers white or lavender
Eriogonum caespitosum	Wild buckwheat	Flowers white, pink, or blue
Eriogonum umbellatum	Sulphur flower	Variable in the basin
Eschscholzia californica	California poppy	Orange flowers
Fritillaria pudica	Yellow bells	Nodding bells in spring
Ipomopsis (Gilia) aggregata	Fairy trumpet	Tubular bells
Lewisia brachycalyx	Lewisia	Moisture in spring
Lewisia nevadensis	Lewisia	Moisture in spring; dry in summer
Penstemon palmeri	Palmer penstemon	Large pink flowers
Penstemon rubicundus	Penstemon	Showy pink blooms
Penstemon speciosus	Showy penstemon	Large blue flowers

and primarily as summer storms in the Chihuahuan Desert. In some areas, no or little rain may fall for two years. Winters are moderate with occasional frost, except in the Mojave, which has cold winters and very hot summers, with extremely high evaporation (causing high water stress for plants).

Soils in the lowest areas are fine-textured, heavy, and often have high concentrations of salts. In the arroyos, or desert washes, soils may be coarse and gravelly. Soil is almost nonexistent in many areas of the rocky desert mountains. Most desert soils are highly alkaline and often have a layer of cementlike caliche at fairly shallow depth, making growth difficult for most plants.

The Mojave Desert, like the nearby Great Basin, is primarily a landscape of low, scattered shrubs. Creosotebush is widespread. The taller Joshua tree occasionally breaks this pattern, as do scattered cacti. Following the winter rains, many annual flowers bloom, forming a low carpet of color in early spring. The plants of the Sonoran Desert are more varied, including the tall saguaro cactus and ocotillo, along with creosotebush and other low shrubs. Arroyos may support some tree growth, particularly paloverde and mesquite. The Chihuahuan Desert is dominated by the low creosotebush, with tarbush, whitethorn acacia, and other shrub companions. These are joined by taller species of yucca, mesquite, and ocotillo in some locations, and by small succulent cacti.

DESERTS
continued

Agave parryi

Opuntia violacea *var.* macrocentra

Ribes odoratum

Baptisia australis

PLANTS OF WARM DESERTS

Latin Name	Common Name	Description
TREES		
Bursera fagaroides	Elephant tree	Resin of this smooth-barked tree was burned as incense in Mayan and Aztec temples; very gnarled and mysterious
Cercidium floridum	Paloverde	Bright green trunk and branches
Olneya tesota	Desert ironwood	Handsome flowers; to 25 feet
Washingtonia filifera	California palm	Beautiful; looks tropical
SHRUBS		
Beloperone californica	Chuparosa	Red flowers that attract hummingbirds
Calliandra eriophylla	Fairy duster	Showy pink to white, fluffy flowers in late winter, early spring
Cassia covesii and C. lindheimerana	Desert senna	Yellow flowers
Chilopsis linearis	Desert catalpa	Attractive flowers; catalpalike pendant pods
Dalea greggii	Indigo bush	Showy rose-purple flowers
Encelia farinosa	Brittlebush	Gum was burned as incense in Baja California churches
Fouquieria splendens	Ocotillo	Spiny desert shrub; showy flowers
Simmondsia chinensis	Jojoba	Beans yield a high-quality oil
Sophora arizonica	Arizona mountain laurel	Fragrant, wisteria-like flowers
Tecoma stans	Yellow trumpetbush	Widely cultivated; used for browse by bighorn sheep

PLANTS OF SOUTHWESTERN GRASSLANDS

Latin Name	Common Name	Description
GRASSES		
Bouteloua eriopoda	Black gramagrass	Important forage species
Hilaria mutica	Tobosa grass	Blue-green; stems to 2 feet
Muhlenbergia porteri	Bush muhly	Feathery inflorescences
ANNUALS AND PERENNIALS		
Abronia	Sand verbena	Showy pink to white flowers; often in dry beds of desert streams
Baileya multiradiata	Desert marigold	Showy yellow daisies on woolly plant
Coreopsis bigelovii	Tickseed	Annual large golden flowers
Eschscholzia mexicana	Gold poppy	Yellow-flowered cousin of California poppy
Lupinus sparsiflorus	Lupine	Violet; many other species; mostly showy
Penstemon eatoni	Firecracker	Tubular scarlet flowers that attract hummingbirds
Penstemon palmeri	Palmer penstemon	Fragrant flowers in pink or lavender
Penstemon parryi	Parry penstemon	Very showy rose flowers
Penstemon pseudospectabilis	Desert penstemon	Pink flowers
Penstemon spectabilis	Penstemon	Lavender-purple; California
Proboscidia althaeifolia	Devil's claw	Very strange large, clawed pods

Latin Name	Common Name	Description
Salvia columbariae	Chia	Source of pinole
Stachys coccinea	Scarlet hedge nettle	Scarlet flowers
Zauschneria latifolia	Hummingbird trumpet	More generous of leaf than the California species, but otherwise similar
Zephyranthes longifolia	Zephyr lily	White or pinkish lilies

PLANTS OF HIGH PLAINS PRAIRIES

Latin Name	Common Name	Description
SHRUBS AND SMALL TREES		
Artemisia tridentata	Big sagebrush	Silver-gray stems; to 10 feet; aromatic
Cercis occidentalis	Redbud	Fruit orange-red to dark purple; to 150 feet
Cercocarpus montanus	Mountain mahogany	Feathery seed plumes in fall
Eurotia lanata	Winter fat	Shrub with whitish woolly foliage
Juniperus scopulorum	Rocky Mountain juniper	Bluish; branches droop, soft foliage; dry, exposed sites
Rhus trilobata	Lemonade sumac	Berries used to make flavored beverage
Ribes odoratum	Golden currant	Yellow flowers have a clovelike fragrance
Sarcobatus vermiculatus	Greasewood	Gray bark, blue-green leaves
GRASSES		
Andropogon gerardii	Big bluestem	Plains strains are shorter than in the prairie proper
Andropogon smithii	Western wheatgrass	
Bouteloua gracilis	Blue gramagrass	Excellent companion for dwarf annuals and perennials
Bouteloua curtipendula	Side-oats grama	Ornamental hanging oats
Buchloe dactyloides	Buffalo grass	Very short species with separate male and female plants
Koeleria cristata	Junegrass	Warm season species that flowers early to midsummer
Schizachyrium scoparium	Little bluestem	Rusty orange fall color
Stipa comata	Needle-and-thread grass	Flowers in summer; to 2 feet or more
ANNUALS AND PERENNIALS		
Allium drummondii	Wild onion	
Amorpha canescens	Leadplant	Shrub with whitish foliage and purple flowers
Anemome patens	Pasque flower	Early purple flowers, showy
Arnica fulgens	Arnica	Flowers golden, plant gray
Asclepias ovalifolia	Oval-leaved milkweed	Subtle; slender stems
Baptisia australis	Blue baptisia	Showy legume
Callirhoe involucrata	Buffalo poppy	Large crimson flowers
Castilleja	Indian paintbrush	Sow seeds around prairie grasses such as *Schizachyrium scoparium*
Coreopsis tinctoria	Tickseed	Annual yellow daisy
Delphinium virescens	Prairie larkspur	Flowers white, sometimes pale blue
Dodecatheon pulchellum	Shooting star	Deep pink blooms; shady sites
Echinacea purpurea	Purple coneflower	Very showy; flower rays are pink
Gaillardia aristata	Blanket flower	Sunburst flowers, widely grown in old-fashioned perennial gardens
Geum triflorum	Prairie smoke	Feathery seed heads
Ipomoea leptophylla	Bigroot bush morning glory	Gigantic tuberous roots; lavender flowers
Leucocrinum montanum	Sand lily	White lilies in spring; plant of alpine form
Liatris punctata	Blazing star	Purple, shorter than Eastern species
Lilium philadelphicum	Prairie lily	Upright orange lilies
Oenothera missourensis	Missouri primrose	Large floppy flowers and great winged seedpods
Pediocactus simpsonii	Small cactus	Pink flowers, to 2 inches across
Penstemon angustifolius	Penstemon	Rich, light blue flowers; many other species available
Psoralea esculenta	Breadroot	Its starchy, tuberous roots were a staple in Plains Indians diets
Ratibida columnifera	Coneflower	Easy to establish; rays yellow or red
Townsendia exscapa and *T. hookeri*	Easter daisies	Stemless rosettes of white daisies
Yucca glauca	Great Plains yucca	Variable, look for especially showy forms

NATURAL GARDENS IN HUMID REGIONS

A rhododendron thrives in a garden that has been allowed to go wild. Sour gum (Nyssa sylvatica), a typical understory tree of eastern hardwood forests, shows its fall leaf color.

A large percentage of the population of North America lives in areas that were once densely forested. These regions receive moderate to heavy precipitation, usually distributed fairly evenly throughout the year. In general, soils in these areas are deep and fertile from their centuries of verdant cover, although in warm areas with heavy rainfall, soils may be depleted of potassium and phosphorous.

Natural forces in moist climates are constantly working to re-create a climax forest through the process of succession. A woodland meadow is a step in the process, analogous to a freeze-frame in time. As plants and their interrelated community mature, they reach toward the next level of their natural evolution.

If your property has many trees, it is a woodland setting ready for your creative garden management. If there are no existing trees and your goal is a woodland setting, you can purchase trees to plant. If you are working within budget constraints, plant some fast-

growing trees for a quick effect and interplant them with slower-growing, longer-lived trees to eventually replace the fast-starters. To avoid overcrowding, establish a schedule for thinning out the temporary trees. Fast-growing, small-to medium-size trees for moist climates include poplar, aspen, wild plum, wild cherry, black locust, and some birches.

In nature, woodlands occur between meadows and the deep forest. In the open meadow low grasses and annuals and perennials thrive in the sun. The edge of the meadow usually abounds in shrubs, ground-covers, and woody perennials. Some of these prefer the dappled shade offered by the light tree cover at the edge of the woodland. Understory shrubs that supply food for wildlife include dogwood, blueberry, azalea, yew, and viburnum.

FOREST WOODLAND PLANTS

The unusual flowers of the tulip tree (Liriodendron) are delightful when viewed up close. The common name comes from the tulip shape of the flower.

planting soil, or add a tablet or two of time-released fertilizer. Create a soil berm, or watering basin, around the tree and mulch it with coarse organic material. During rainy weather, cut a hole in the berm so that excess rainwater can drain away from the root ball.

A selection guide to small trees to plant in your forest woodland begins on page 41. Some of these will adapt in any North American forest region. See the map on page 17 for your specific location.

FOREST WOODLAND TREES

Small trees are part of the woodland landscape. Many species are excellent as background plants in the natural garden or as individual specimens to shade your patio or deck. In nature, woodland trees often grow above an understory of shrubs and perennials.

Many trees listed here have an open structure and cast dappled shade, allowing a variety of plants to grow beneath them. Others offer flowers and fruit, providing food as well as shelter for wildlife. In natural woodland settings they grow in clusters or groups and only rarely as individual specimens. Plant small groups of the species you enjoy most.

Use woodlands as a background to screen out unpleasant views or to create privacy. Trees also make effective windbreaks. Leave some open spaces for interest between background trees. Plant tall species in locations that won't block attractive views.

Forest woodland trees appreciate fertilizer at planting time, followed by annual fertilizing after they are established. When planting, mix a granulated fertilizer with the

FOREST WOODLAND SHRUBS

Many shrubs native to the forest regions of North America will thrive in your forest woodland garden. A grouping of these plants provides varied interest and requires almost no maintenance.

Woodland gardens in forest regions require an open-textured soil that is rich in humus and slightly acidic. The soil should drain quickly. Some forest shrubs and perennials—notably azaleas and blueberries—require soil that is more than slightly acidic. Fertilize these selectively with a balanced fertilizer made for acid-loving plants. You can help keep the soil in the correct pH range by adding composted leaves to the planting soil or using them as mulch.

In general, fall planting of shrubs is best, but early spring planting is also acceptable. When planting under existing trees or near large established shrubs, dig large holes and fill them with rich planting soil so that the new shrubs will have a chance to grow.

FOREST WOODLAND PLANTS
continued

Fothergilla is a midspring bloomer. Flowers and fall color are best in light shade.

Crimson petals of fire pink (Silene virginica) appear in late summer.

White bunchberry flowers are followed by red berries in fall.

FOREST WOODLAND GROUNDCOVERS

In some settings groundcovers are excellent replacements for a lawn. In fact, in some municipalities an infrequently mowed meadow is not acceptable as a front yard, whereas a ground cover is. Once established, groundcovers require little maintenance and serve the same kinds of visual landscape functions as lawns do—that is, to form a low foreground for other elements in the landscape such as flower beds, shrubs, or foundation plantings.

On the other hand, the spreading nature of groundcovers can make them invasive or garden thugs (see page 78) in the wrong setting. Check with local nursery professionals or extension service advisers for groundcovers that will not overwhelm the landscape.

Many kinds of plants— low shrubs, vines, and perennials—can be used as groundcovers. Plants that look at home in an open woodland glade will serve a similar function as part of a residential landscape. An example is periwinkle (*Vinca minor*), a low plant that roots at the stem joints as it spreads. It has rounded, dark green leaves and blue-purple flowers throughout most of the spring and into the summer. It grows in sun or partial shade and is hardy in most regions of North America. It is not difficult to keep from spreading, yet it grows thickly enough to discourage other plants from entering its territory. Maintenance is reduced to an absolute minimum once the planting is established. Periwinkle can be mowed to 6 inches in fall to keep it from piling upon itself and creating mounds. It is hardy to Zone 4.

Plant bulbs, such as narcissus and daffodils, to poke through periwinkle from below and scatter a delight of spring flowers across the dark green blanket. Gently pry apart the creeping periwinkle stems, dig a hole about a foot in diameter, and enrich the soil with compost and fertilizer. Place five or six bulbs in each hole.

Another low groundcover that naturalizes under trees (even pines) is Japanese spurge. In cool, moist climates it will grow in full sun as well as shade. Its leaves are saw-toothed and a rich, dark green (paler in full sun). It fills in thickly and will not let other low plants grow within its boundaries. Once established it handles moderate drought and requires almost no maintenance. It is hardy to Zone 4.

Carpet bugle is a low groundcover with purple-blue flower spikes and glossy leaves. It prefers partial shade and grows best in a woodland setting along paths or under the cover of open trees, where the shade is dappled. It will allow clumps of spring bulbs and small shrubs such as azalea or daphne to grow up through it. Flat stepping-stones through a field of carpet bugle make a delightful woodland path. This plant is hardy to Zone 4.

Bluebell (*Campanula rotundifolia*) is a delicate, low meadow plant that blooms throughout the summer and is suited to moist eastern climates. It is hardy in Zones 2 through 7.

FOREST WOODLAND PERENNIALS

Herbaceous perennials are soft-stemmed plants with generally faster growth and shorter lives than woody stemmed shrubs. In nature, they grow in the company of trees, shrubs, and grasses. When clearings occur in the forest or woodland, perennials, along with annual plants, are the first to appear in nature's succession.

Many perennials are free flowering. They bring color, fragrance, and grace to the landscape. Perennials are long-term additions to the garden. They may die back to the ground in winter in cold climates but reappear in spring. Some reproduce themselves easily, lasting for many years in the same location.

Buy perennials at local or mail-order nurseries or propagate them by cuttings, rhizomes, or seeds and naturalize easily in a meadow or at the woodland edge among the trees and shrubs. The plants listed on subsequent pages are mostly native to the eastern United States and will grow there with little maintenance. After some period of time to become established, most prefer to be left completely alone. In addition, most attract and help support native wildlife.

PLANTS OF EASTERN FORESTS

Latin Name	Common Name	Description
TREES		
Acer rubrum	Red maple	Brilliant orange and scarlet fall color; streamsides to upland forests
Acer saccharum	Sugar maple	Orange fall color; excellent, long-lived shade tree
Betula papyrifera	Paper birch	White, papery bark; light yellow fall color
Carya ovata	Shagbark hickory	Gray bark peels in 1- to 3-inch slender strips; hickory nut of commerce
Liriodendron tulipifera	Tulip poplar	Large shade tree; tulip-shaped leaves and flowers
Pinus strobus	Eastern white pine	Large, 5-needle pine; excellent for windbreaks
Quercus alba	White oak	Large, slow-growing species; maroon fall color
Quercus coccinea	Scarlet oak	Small red oak with brilliant scarlet fall color
Quercus stellata	Post oak	Fall color dull yellow to brown; gravelly or sandy uplands
Tsuga canadensis	Hemlock	Cone-shaped, large evergreen; branches pendulous; cones less than 1 inch long
SHRUBS		
Amelanchier laevis	Allegheny shadblow	Small tree with showy white flowers in spring and purple to blackish berries in late summer
Aristolochia durior	Dutchman's pipe	Vine with curious pipelike flowers
Chionanthus virginicus	Fringe tree	Large shrub or small tree with greenish flowers and blue or black fruit; mostly on stream banks
Cornus florida	Flowering dogwood	Small tree with very showy flowers
Fothergilla major	Large fothergilla	Profuse white flowers in spring, sweetly fragrant
Hamamelis virginiana	Witch hazel	Yellow flowers in fall
Viburnum prunifolium	Black haw	Shrub to small tree with white flowers and dark blue fruit; brilliant scarlet fall color
Viburnum trilobum	Highbush cranberry	Handsome shrub with large red berries
FERNS		
Adiantum pedatum	Maidenhair fern	Elegant fern with leaflets branching from 1- to 2-foot wiry stem
Osmunda cinnamomea	Cinnamon fern	Fronds turn cinnamon brown as spores ripen
Osmunda claytoniana	Interrupted fern	Edible fiddleheads
ANNUALS AND PERENNIALS		
Asarum canadense	Wild ginger	Reddish flowers that hide under heart-shaped leaves; excellent ground cover
Chrysogonum virginianum	Chrysogonum	Yellow daisy that blooms all summer
Cornus canadensis	Bunchberry	Groundcover with white dogwood flowers and red berries
Epigaea repens	Trailing arbutus	Showy groundcover; grows in moist peaty soils
Erythronium americanum	Trout lily	Handsome yellow lily
Hepatica acutiloba and H. americana	Hepatica	Leaves in 3 parts; masses of flowers in white to rose to lavender
Iris cristata	Dwarf crested iris	Handsome, purple-flowered species
Jeffersonia diphylla	Twinleaf	Leaves resemble butterflies
Mertensia virginica	Virginia bluebell	Clusters of hanging flowers
Mitchella repens	Partridgeberry	White flowers; red berries
Phlox divaricata and P. stolonifera	Phlox	Light blue and red, respectively
Polygonatum biflorum	Solomon's seal	Tall, lilylike stems with blue berries
Sanguinaria canadensis	Bloodroot	One of earliest woodland plants to bloom
Shortia galacifolia	Oconee bell	Choice woodland plant; white, pink, or blue flowers
Silene virginica	Fire pink	Five scarlet petals in star formation
Smilacina stellata	Starry false Solomon's seal	Similar to Solomon's seal
Trillium	Trillium	Single stem with 3 leaves and 3-petalled white, pink, or maroon flower

**Red oak
(Quercus rubra)
thrives in the
Midwest.**

**Red berries
of Viburnum
trilobum.**

**Staghorn sumac
(Rhus typhina)
colors brilliantly
in fall.**

PLANTS OF NORTHERN FORESTS

Latin Name	Common Name	Description
TREES		
Acer saccharum	Sugar maple	Widely planted for shade and bright orange-red fall color
Alnus rugosa	Speckled alder	Small with showy catkins and cones
Amelanchier canadensis	Serviceberry	Earliest *Amelanchier* to blossom
Betula lutea	Yellow birch	Peeling, yellowish bark; often on river floodplains
Carpinus caroliniana	Blue beech	Grayish bark; bright scarlet and orange fall color
Carya ovata	Shagbark hickory	Large, with edible nuts; grows in uplands with oaks
Cornus alternifolia	Pagoda dogwood	Small flat-topped trees; branches in pagodalike tiers; yellow and scarlet fall color
Crataegus crus-galli	Hawthorn	Edible red berries; often grows at edge of forest and meadow
Diervilla lonicera	Dwarf honeysuckle	Yellow clusters of flowers; small shrub
Euonymus atropurpurea	Wahoo	Relative of bittersweet; bright red clusters of hanging capsules in fall
Fagus grandifolia	American beech	Smooth gray bark; often with sugar maple and tulip tree
Fraxinus americana	White ash	Yellow or purple fall color; on rich soils of bottomlands
Gleditsia triacanthos inermis	Honey locust	Long, twisted seedpods; pale yellow fall color
Gymnocladus dioica	Kentucky coffee tree	Short, heavy seedpods; ground for coffee substitute in 18th and 19th centuries
Hamamelis virginiana	Witch hazel	Yellow flowers in fall
Larix laricina	Tamarack	Pyramidal, deciduous conifer; wide range of habitats from uplands to swamps
Liriodendron tulipifera	Tulip tree	Tall and straight, with fissured bark and tuliplike leaves and flowers
Malus coronaria	Crabapple	Showy pink to white flowers; small yellow-green apples
Ostrya virginiana	Ironwood	Understory tree; elmlike leaves; yellow fall color
Physocarpus opulifolius	Ninebark	Spirealike shrubs with exfoliating bark
Pinus resinosa	Red pine	Reddish bark and 2-inch cones
Pinus strobus	Eastern white pine	Large, 5-needle pine; widely planted
Plantanus occidentalis	Sycamore	Distinctive plated bark; often branches into several trunks
Prunus americana	Wild plum	Showy white to pink flowers; bright red fruit
Prunus serotina	Wild black cherry	Large with plated bark; yellow fall color
Quercus alba	Upland white oak	Very large and slow-growing; deep red fall color
Quercus bicolor	Swamp white oak	Large, fast-growing; yellow to orange fall color
Quercus rubra	Red oak	Large and fast-growing skyline tree
Rhus typhina	Staghorn sumac	Cinnamon brown fruit clusters; intense scarlet fall color
Tilia americana	Basswood	Large and excellent for shade; yellow fall color
Tsuga canadensis	Hemlock	Large, pyramidal evergreen; drooping branches; small cones
SHRUBS		
Actaea pachypoda	Baneberry	2- to 3-foot plants with showy berries in fall
Viburnum lentago	Nannyberry	Dark blue berries; orange to red fall color
Viburnum trilobum	Highbush cranberry	Large red berries
ANNUALS AND PERENNIALS		
Anemonella thalictroides	Rue anemone	Delicate white anemones in early spring
Aquilegia canadensis	Columbine	Attractive hanging yellow and red flowers in summer
Arisaema atrorubens	Jack-in-the-pulpit	Showy, unusual flowers; bright scarlet fruit clusters in fall
Asarum canadense	Wild ginger	Excellent groundcover with heart-shaped leaves
Aster macrophyllus	Big-leaved aster	Subtle; leaves very large and basal
Erythronium	Trout lily	White and yellow flowers on 4- to 8-inch stems
Hepatica acutiloba	Hepatica	Leathery leaves and white, pink, blue, or purple flowers
Mertensia virginica	Virginia bluebell	Hanging bell-shaped blue flowers; sun or light shade

PLANTS OF PACIFIC FORESTS

Latin Name	Common Name	Description
TREES		
Abies concolor	White fir	Large; frequently planted; bears upright cones
Acer macrophyllum	Big-leaf maple	Large, deeply divided leaves; bright yellow fall color
Alnus rubra and A. rhombifolia	Alder	30- to 40-foot trees with grayish bark; on stream banks
Calocedrus decurrens	Incense cedar	Tall tapering evergreen; 100–150 feet; widely planted
Chamaecyparis lawsoniana	Port Orford cedar	To 200 feet; widely planted; natural groves near coasts
Cornus nuttallii	Pacific dogwood	40–60 feet; white-pink petals to 3 inches long, scarlet berries
Lithocarpus densiflorus	Tanbark oak	80–150 feet; abundant in coastal redwood belt
Pinus lambertiana	Sugar pine	200-foot pyramidal tree; large cones to 18 inches long
Pinus monticola	Western white pine	100–150 feet; cones to 11 inches
Pinus ponderosa	Ponderosa pine	To 230 feet; cinnamon-red bark; widely planted
Pseudotsuga menziesii	Douglas fir	To 200 feet; blue-green foliage
Quercus agrifolia	Coast live oak	To 90 feet; leaves oval, toothed; acorns to 1½ inches long
Quercus chrysolepis	Canyon live oak	To 50 feet; horizontal branches; evergreen
Quercus garryana	Oregon post oak	Deciduous tree to 60 feet
Quercus kelloggii	California black oak	To 100 feet; yellow or brown fall color; acorns to 1½ inches
Sequoia sempervirens	Redwood	To 340 feet; widely planted; cones very small
Tsuga mertensiana	Mountain hemlock	To 150 feet; drooping branches; oval, cylindric cones
Umbellularia californica	California bay	75–150 feet; aromatic leaves yellow to orange in fall
SHRUBS		
Acer circinatum	Vine maple	30–40 feet; rich orange to scarlet fall color
Amelanchier alnifolia	Saskatoon berry	To 20 feet; white flowers in spring; fruit dark blue and edible
Corylus cornuta californica	Hazel	To 15 feet; needs moisture
Garrya fremontii	Silk tassel bush	Hanging clusters of male and female flowers; to 10 feet
Gaultheria shallon	Salal	Small with shiny green leaves; urnlike flowers in clusters
Holodiscus discolor	Oceanspray	To 15 feet; dense clusters of small white to pink flowers
Physocarpus capitatus	Ninebark	Peeling bark, white flowers
Rhamnus purshiana	Cascara	To 40 feet; deciduous; yellow fall color; in rich coniferous forest
Rhododendron macrophyllum	California rosebay	Clusters of rose-purple flowers; leaves to 9 inches long
Rhododendron occidentale	Western azalea	To 15 feet; clusters of showy white flowers
Ribes sanguineum	Red flowering currant	12 feet; flowers pale to deep rose; dark berries
Vaccinium ovatum	Evergreen huckleberry	6 feet; flowers white to pink; black berries
FERNS		
Adiantum pedatum	Maidenhair fern	Delicate fronds on 1- to 2-foot stalk
Asplenium trichomanes	Spleenwort	Small woodland fern
Athyrium filix-femina	Lady fern	Large, showy fern with both coastal and mountain varieties
Polystichum munitum	Sword fern	Showy, dark green fern; abundant under redwoods
Woodwardia fimbriata	Chain fern	Large handsome species; needs moist conditions
ANNUALS AND PERENNIALS		
Aconitum columbianum	Monkshood	Dark blue flowers on 3- to 5-foot stalks; similar to delphinium
Aquilegia formosa	Columbine	Edge and moist woods; red and yellow hanging flowers
Asarum caudatum	Wild ginger	Shade-tolerant groundcover
Clintonia uniflora	Queen's cup	Large, oval basal leaves; small white flowers and blue berries
Dicentra formosa	Bleeding heart	Rose flowers and fernlike foliage; coastal
Erythronium oregonum	Fawn lily	Flowers pink outside and yellow or rose within
Linnaea borealis	Twinflower	Excellent groundcover
Smilacina racemosa	False Solomon's seal	Terminal clusters of bright red berries in fall
Trillium grandiflorum	Trillium	Flowers white aging to pink; T. rivale is tiny
Vancouveria species	Inside-out flower	Fernlike plants with white flowers (yellow in V. chrysantha)

High humidity and more than 200 inches of rain per year create a lush green carpet in the Hoh rain forest of Olympic National Park in Washington State.

Strong muscular trunks are just one reason yellowwood is a beautiful year-round tree.

Round-lobed hepatica has leathery, liver-shaped leaves and delicate light blue flowers.

Trillium, phlox, and foamflower combine to make an attractive landscape groundcover.

PLANTS OF CENTRAL FORESTS

Latin Name	Common Name	Description
TREES		
Acer rubrum	Red maple	Tends to occur on wetter sites
Acer saccharum	Sugar maple	Especially with beech and basswood
Aesculus glabra	Ohio buckeye	Excellent shade tree
Betula lutea	Yellow birch	Especially on wetter sites
Carpinus caroliniana	Blue beech	Small tree with smooth grayish bark
Carya	Hickory	Present but not dominant in central Appalachians
Cladrastis lutea	Yellowwood	Foot-long clusters of white, pea-shaped flowers
Fagus grandifolia	American beech	Stately tree with smooth, gray bark; dominant in much of the Central Deciduous Forest
Fraxinus americana	White ash	Excellent shade tree
Liriodendron tulipifera	Tulip tree	Large tree with tuliplike green and yellow flowers
Quercus shumardii	Shumard oak	Large red oak; excellent for shade
Quercus stellata	Post oak	Medium-size upland white oak; also in deep South
Tilia americana	Basswood	Especially common in beech-maple forest
SHRUBS		
Crataegus marshallii	Parsley hawthorn	Also in deep South
Crataegus opaca	Mayhaw	Showy red fruits; also in deep South
ANNUALS AND PERENNIALS		
Actaea pachypoda and A. rubra	Baneberry	Autumn fruit very showy
Anemonella thalictroides	Rue anemone	Delicate white flowers
Aquilegia canadensis	Wild columbine	Yellow and red flowers
Asarum canadense	Wild ginger	Excellent groundcover
Asarum shuttleworthii	Mottled wild ginger	Leaves mottled with white
Astilbe biternata	False goatsbeard	Feathery white flowers; to 6 feet tall
Hepatica americana	Round-lobed hepatica	Very early May baskets of white, rose, or purple flowers
Iris verna	Vernal iris	Usually in acid soils; the smallest native iris
Isopyrum biternatum	False rue anemone	Forms large mats on the forest floor; delicate anemone flowers; dissected foliage
Jeffersonia diphylla	Twinleaf	Named for Thomas Jefferson; south only to Virginia
Mertensia virginica	Virginia bluebell	Also in sunny meadows
Phlox divaricata	Woodland phlox	Blue flowers
Podophyllum peltatum	Mayapple	Looks like an umbrella; solitary white flower produces large green berry
Sanguinaria canadensis	Bloodroot	Very early white flowers with yellow centers
Shortia galacifolia	Oconee bell	Limited in natural range but very choice in the woodland garden
Tiarella cordifolia	Allegheny foamflower	Fluffy white wands from rosettes of scalloped round leaves; south only to North Carolina
Trillium	Trillium	A vernal visual feast in white, maroon, and pink
Uvularia grandiflora	Bellflower	Pendant yellow flowers in spring
Viola pedata	Bird's-foot violet	Sun or light shade

PLANTS OF SOUTHERN FORESTS

Latin Name	Common Name	Description
TREES		
Carya illinoiensis	Pecan	Edible nuts; to 150 feet
Carya tomentosa	Mockernut hickory	Handsome shade tree
Cercis canadensis	Redbud	Beautiful spring flowers
Cornus florida	Dogwood	Widely planted native
Franklinia altamaha	Franklinia	Tree in camellia family extinct in the wild since 1806; named for Benjamin Franklin
Ilex cassine	Cassine holly	Pale green foliage; large shrub to small tree
Ilex opaca	American holly	Bright red berries; pyramidal form
Juniperus virginiana	Eastern red cedar	Excellent for impoverished soils
Liquidambar styraciflua	American sweet gum	Showy autumn colors, depending on cultivar; pendant, spiny spherical fruits
Magnolia acuminata	Cucumber magnolia	Flowers greenish; excellent shade tree
Magnolia grandiflora	Southern magnolia	White flowers to 8 inches across; shiny, dark evergreen leaves
Magnolia macrophylla	Big-leaf magnolia	Leaves to 2½ feet long, 12 inches wide; flowers to 15 inches across; deciduous
Magnolia virginiana	Sweet bay magnolia	Flowers white and lemon scented; semievergreen
Nyssa sylvatica	Black gum	Early scarlet fall color; alligator bark
Oxydendrum arboreum	Sourwood	Fragrant flowers resemble lily-of-the-valley
Persea borbonia	Red bay	Aromatic evergreen leaves used as cooking spice; relative of avocado
Pinus echinata	Shortleaf pine	Fairly fast-growing; plated bark on older specimens
Pinus elliottii	Slash pine	Grows on the poorest soil
Pinus palustris	Longleaf pine	Plumelike foliage; cones to 12 inches
Pinus taeda	Loblolly pine	Fast-growing; pioneer species; excellent shade for azaleas and dogwoods
Prunus caroliniana	Cherry laurel	Evergreen cherry; fruit attracts birds
Quercus alba	White oak	Large, slow-growing species
Quercus falcata	Southern red oak	Popular shade tree in South; provides red fall color
Quercus nigra	Water oak	Tolerant of wide variety of soil conditions
Quercus phellos	Willow oak	Leaves like a willow
Quercus virginiana	Southern live oak	Quintessential tree of the South
Sabal palmetto	Cabbage palm	Hardy only in the deep South; Florida state tree; edible young buds
SHRUBS AND VINES		
Callicarpa americana	American beautyberry	Iridescent purple berries persist after leaves drop
Calycanthus floridus	Carolina allspice	Aromatic foliage; reddish brown flowers
Clematis virginiana	Clematis	Flowers white; male and female flowers on separate plants
Fothergilla major	Large fothergilla	Fluffy white late-spring blooms with honeylike fragrance
Hydrangea quercifolia	Oakleaf hydrangea	Glorious red to purple autumn color
Ilex vomitoria	Yaupon	Translucent hollyberries; multiple stems produce sculptured form
Myrica cerifera	Southern wax myrtle	Fast and dense growth make for excellent hedging plant
Passiflora incarnata	Passionflower	Vine with exotic flowers; host plant of Gulf Fritillary butterfly
Rhododendron austrinum and R. canescens	Flame azalea and wild honeysuckle	Need sun or partial shade; flowers yellow-orange and pink, respectively
Smilax lanceolata	Lanceleaf greenbriar	Vine; used for trellising and cut foliage in bouquets
Wisteria macrostachya	Wisteria	Vine; lavender flowers; large pendant fruits

Oakleaf hydrangea can reach 6 feet high and 8 feet wide.

Carolina allspice can grow to 8 feet tall and is cultivated for its unusual strawberry-scented flowers.

Blooming dogwood trees grace a forest of oak and hickory.

NATURAL GARDENS OF THE EASTERN PRAIRIES

Grasses mixed with wildflowers make up prairies. In spring this landscape is dominated by a mix of various types of green grasses and dotted with colorful flowers, sometimes masses of them. During summer and fall the grasses turn to shades of yellow, tan, and golden brown; the mix of flowers changes as some go to seed and others come into bloom.

Prairies once covered vast areas of the dry Midwest, but agriculture has supplanted all but small portions of this type of landscape. People lucky enough to have seen the prairies' gracefully swaying flower spikes and seed plumes never forget it.

A prairie in your front yard will exhibit stunning changes throughout the growing season. Brilliant green spikes of grass appear in spring and then are joined by colorful wildflowers that bloom all summer. In fall the golden seed plumes keep company with more subdued fall blossoms. These changes identify the seasons clearly and with charm.

Prairie plants survive the dry summers of their native habitat by sending their roots deep into the soil for available water. Once established, these plants are stable and long-lived and need very little maintenance, an important bonus for your own prairie garden.

Bee balm, a native of the the Eastern Prairie, combines perfectly here with exotics such as yarrow (Achillea), hollyhock (Alcea), and Russian sage (Perovskia atriplicifolia).

Yellow prairie coneflower (Ratibida), purple spikes of blazing star (Liatris), and white umbels of Queen Anne's lace (Daucus) combine with native grasses in this restored Wisconsin tall-grass prairie.

TALL-GRASS PRAIRIE

In a broad band along the western edge of the Eastern Deciduous Forests, from the eastern plains of Alberta to Texas, were once the tall-grass prairies. Historically this region included much of the states of Nebraska, Iowa, Kansas, Missouri, Illinois, and Indiana. This is the richest part of the great grassland, a nearly flat region that rises from the eastern forests to the western plains, a region of deep, fertile soils and grasses as tall as a man on a horse.

Little of the tall-grass prairie now remains, having given way to the cultivated grasslands of corn, wheat, and other crops.

Annual rainfall is lower here than in the adjacent forests and steadily decreases toward the west. Amounts vary from 40 inches in the east to 15 inches in the short-grass plains of the west, and it comes mainly as summer rain. Plants here must adapt to summer water stress. Both east and west, winters can be very cold and summers very hot with drying winds. Soils are

Pasque flower (above, right) complements vetch. Grasses of tall-grass prairie combine with tall-growing, flowering perennials (left).

NATURAL GARDENS OF THE EASTERN PRAIRIES
continued

A shallow water bowl surrounded by nectar-rich plants is an attraction butterflies can't resist.

heavier than in the forests and lower in some nutrients.

The appearance of the tall-grass prairie changes from spring to fall. In spring and early summer, plants such as compass plant send up tall flowering stalks and dominate with their showy blooms. Gradually the grasses (including big bluestem, Indiangrass, and others) grow taller than the flowering plants, and in mid- to late summer their flowering stems can reach heights of 10 feet or more.

Extensive areas of tall-grass prairie alternating with belts of forest form an area called the prairie parkland, a transition zone between grassland and forest that extends from Alberta through Illinois, Missouri, Kansas, and Oklahoma, and to the Gulf Coast. The trees of this region include oak, hickory, and, in the north, aspen. At the southern edge of the tall-grass prairie is the prairie brushland of Texas, where mesquite, live oak, and juniper blend with the grasses.

In eastern Nebraska and Kansas and in the uplands of Iowa, taller and shorter grasses intermingle in a transition zone between the tall-grass prairie and short-grass plains.

PRAIRIE PLANTS: In the eastern United States and southeastern Canada, a few native grasses have proven themselves effective in combination with one another and with wildflowers. These are side-oats grama (*Bouteloua curtipendula*), Junegrass (*Koeleria pyramidata*), switch grass (*Panicum virgatum*), northern dropseed (*Sporobolus heterolepis*), and little bluestem (*Schizachyrium scoparium*). Plant these grasses as plugs or sow seed in early May.

Some nonnative, low-growing fescue grasses (*Festuca ovina* and *F. longifolia*) might also work, but if they are too well-adapted to your climate, they can grow thick enough to crowd out wildflowers.

Grasses will take two to three years to become established in your prairie. During this time keep them mowed to a height of 8 inches; this will cause them to thicken. Pull out any undesirable weeds that begin to encroach. After several years let the meadow grow until fall and then mow it once to about 5 inches. Because a meadow is just the first stage in the succession toward a forest, it will be necessary to temporarily freeze the process in order to maintain open space.

Although annual mowing helps do this, it might also be necessary to remove seedlings of shrubs and trees trying to establish themselves in the space you prefer to keep open.

Different plants from those mentioned above are used in the warmer and more humid southeastern United States. Grasses that have been proven in that climate are broomsedge (*Andropogon virginicus*), bushy bluestem (*Schizachyrium gomeratus*), silver broomsedge (*Andropogon ternarius*), purple muhly (*Muhlenbergia capallaris*), Indian grass (*Sorghastrum nutans*), switchgrass, and purple love grass (*Eragrostis spectabilis*). Always sow a mixture of grass seed to encourage the development of a diversified community. Soil and moisture conditions, as well as the amount of sun, will dictate which species, if any, become dominant.

In the southern United States, wildflowers turn brown by midsummer. Plan on one mowing in June, when the spring wildflowers have finished their show. Mow again in August or early September to clean up the stragglers. Another mowing in December may be warranted if you decide that the landscape looks too rough and unkempt.

Grasses should make up about 75 percent of the meadow plant community, with wildflowers making up no more than 25 percent. Nature will determine the actual percentages after you have done the seeding. Each site has its own particular conditions, so the results are not entirely predictable. In addition, changes will occur over the years. Some wildflower species will disappear from your meadow as others proliferate.

CONVERTING TO PRAIRIE

Till organic amendment into soil, incorporating it to a depth of 4 to 6 inches. Do this by hand with a shovel in small areas, but consider a power tiller for large areas.

You can convert a maintained turf of domesticated lawn grasses into meadow, but not by letting it go wild. Instead, eliminate the existing lawn completely by smothering it and starting over. The reason is that a lawn won't naturalize well by itself, especially if you live near an agricultural area where there are thistles (*Cirsium*), purple ragweed (*Ambrosia*), loosestrife, or other undesirable invasive plants.

If your existing lawn area is small, covering it with black plastic or some other opaque material will smother the existing grasses and kill germinating weed seeds. Leave the plastic material on the area through the fall and winter and then thoroughly till the soil before replanting in spring.

The tilling method of eradicating existing grasses is a lot more work. The area must be tilled a number of times, each a week apart, or the existing plants will reroot and resprout. Eradicating tough grasses that spread by rhizomes could require repeated tillings through several growing seasons.

Turfing out a large area of existing lawn requires mechanical equipment. A sod cutter, available through rental centers, strips off the existing turf. Then the bare soil can be prepared by tilling. A layer of organic material up to 2 inches deep may be added to the soil at the time it is tilled. The removed turf can be stacked in a shady spot, where it will slowly turn to an excellent compost.

Turfing out will not work with deep-rooted grasses such as bermudagrass, which will resprout from the roots left in the soil and become a persistent weed in the new meadow. The bermudagrass should be killed before it is removed. Spray the lawn twice with a glyphosate-based herbicide, which will kill all the weeds and grass. One week after application, water. A week later spray again. You can remove the dead grass or till it under. Although the grass will still be green, the roots will not resprout. Glyphosate breaks down in the soil in a few days and has no effect on future plantings.

Before you plant a new garden bed, improve the soil by spreading several inches of organic matter over the surface. Then till or spade the organic matter into the top 6 inches of soil. Avoid tilling or spading when the soil is wet.

Annual flowers such as pink and white phlox, blue cornflower (Centaurea), red and pink poppy (Papaver), and golden cosmos predominate in the first season of this meadow. Over time, blooms of perennial flowers will increase.

PLANTS OF PRAIRIES IN HUMID REGIONS

Many varieties of the native North American prairie plant bee balm (Monardia didyma), are available. This one is 'Garden View Scarlet'.

Fall flowers of native New England aster (Aster novae-angliae 'Wood's Pink') look refined enough for any home garden border.

The massive, rose-purple clusters of Joe-Pye weed 'Gateway' (right) bloom profusely on 6-foot mottled stems.

In June this stretch of virgin prairie is abloom with shooting stars and orange puccoon. Here, in July, Liatris pichifolia dominates.

PLANTS OF PRAIRIES IN HUMID REGIONS

Latin Name	Common Name	Description
GRASSES		
Andropogon virginicus	Broom sedge	Similar to little bluestem; not as colorful in fall
Bouteloua curtipendula	Side-oats grama	2–3 feet; some are sod-formers; others cluster in bunches
Koeleria cristata	Junegrass	Showy inflorescences; glossy spikelike panicles
Schizachyrium scoparium	Little bluestem	2–3 feet; rusty orange fall color
ANNUALS AND PERENNIALS		
Asclepias tuberosa	Butterfly weed	Bright orange flowers
Aster novae-angliae	New England aster	Showy purple flowers with yellow centers
Baptisia australis	Blue baptisia	Large blue pealike flowers
Baptisia tinctoria	Yellow baptisia	Showy yellow flowers; 2–3 feet
Bidens aristosa	Western tickseed	Showy yellow sunflowers with yellow centers; prefers wet meadows
Coreopsis lanceolata	Lance-leaved coreopsis	1–2 feet; bright yellow flowers; dry or sandy soils
Dodecatheon meadia	Shooting star	Clusters of showy flowers with bright pink reflexed petals
Echinacea purpurea	Purple coneflower	Purple daisies
Eryngium yuccifolium	Rattlesnake-master	Leaves like a yucca; umbels of spherical white flower clusters
Eupatorium maculatum and E. purpureum	Joe-Pye weed	Purple flowers
Filipendula rubra	Queen-of-the-prairie	Very showy clusters of delicate pink flowers
Iris versicolor	Wild blue flag	Blue flowers; 3 feet tall
Krigia biflora	Two-flowered Cynthia	Flowers deep orange; leaves glaucous, mostly basal, and blue-green
Liatris pycnostachya	Prairie gayfeather	Purple spikes of this and the similar L. spicata can be bought as cut flowers
Lilium canadense	Wild yellow lily	Orange-yellow to red-spotted flowers
Lilium martagon	Turk's-cap lily	Purple flowers spotted with black
Lilium michiganense	Michigan lily	Whorled leaves; orange-red spotted flowers
Lilium philadelphicum	Prairie or wood lily	Showy yellow and red-orange flowers
Lupinus perennis	Lupine	Showy bluish flowers
Mertensia virginica	Virginia bluebell	In meadows and woods; blooms when morels are up
Monarda didyma	Scarlet bee balm	Showy scarlet pompoms
Monarda fistulosa	Wild bergamot	Lavender flowers; plants aromatic
Rhexia mariana and R. virginica	Meadow beauty	Flowers pale pink and deep, vivid pink respectively; very beautiful
Rudbeckia triloba	Thin-leaved coneflower	Showy clusters of small, golden sunflowers
Solidago nemoralis	Oldfield goldenrod	Soft golden flowers
Solidago speciosa	Showy goldenrod	Produces golden plumes in late fall
Veronicastrum virginicum	Culver's root	Flowers are slender clusters of vertical white spires
Viola pedata	Bird's-foot violet	Choice dwarf pansy but only for dry, sterile soils
Zizia aurea	Golden Alexander	Showy yellow umbels

Red bee balm, a prairie native (left)*, foils silvery wormwood* (Artemisia) *in the foreground. Fall blooming goldenrod* (right) *contrasts with lavender mallow.*

PLANTS OF NORTHERN PRAIRIES, HUMID REGIONS

Purple coneflower is a staple because of its success in attracting swallowtails and other butterflies.

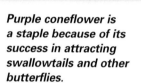

Feathery pink, cotton-candy plumes of Filipendula rubra 'Venusta'.

PLANTS OF NORTHERN PRAIRIES, HUMID REGIONS

Latin Name	Common Name	Description
SHRUBS		
Amorpha canescens	Lead plant	Ash-colored foliage; flowers purple with yellow stamens
Ceanothus americanus	New Jersey tea	To 4 feet; clusters of feathery white flowers
GRASSES		
Andropogon gerardii	Big bluestem	Dominant species; to 6 feet in autumn; yellow, brown, and orange fall colors
Bouteloua curtipendula	Side-oats grama	Dry sites; to 3 feet; buffy fall color
Bouteloua gracilis	Blue gramagrass	Stems in dense, erect clusters; to 20 inches
Elymus canadensis	Nodding Canada wild rye	Easy to establish; showy ryelike heads
Koeleria cristata	Junegrass	Warm season grass; to 18 inches; heads like timothy
Panicum virgatum	Switchgrass	Tall and aggressive; avoid overplanting
Schizachyrium scoparium	Little bluestem	Dry sites; to 3 feet; reddish fall color
Sorghastrum nutans	Indiangrass	Dominant species; to 6 feet in autumn, with cinnamon heads
Sporobolus heterolepis	Northern dropseed	Often considered the most beautiful prairie grass
Stipa spartea	Needlegrass	Warm season grass; to 3½ feet; sharp head of seed gives it its name
ANNUALS AND PERENNIALS		
Asclepias sullivantii	Sullivant's milkweed	Waxy bluish green leaves with pink midveins; pink flowers
Asclepias tuberosa	Butterfly weed	To 3 feet; showy orange flowers; long in cultivation
Asclepias verticillata	Horsetail milkweed	Showy flowers; easy to cultivate
Aster azureus	Sky blue aster	Light blue flowers, to 3 feet; arrow-shaped leaves
Aster laevis	Smooth aster	Smooth shiny leaves; light blue flowers with yellow centers; to 4 feet
Baptisia leucantha	White false indigo	To 4 feet; bearing tall white banners of white pea flowers
Baptisia leucophaea	Cream false indigo	Low clumps to 2 feet tall; yellow pea flowers in low, lateral clusters; very showy
Cacalia tuberosa	Indian plantain	4–5 feet; sparse foliage; light green, shiny leaves
Camassia scilloides	Prairie hyacinth	Spring-blooming bulb producing light purple flowers
Coreopsis palmata	Prairie tickseed	To 2 feet; yellow daisies with yellow centers; forms large clumps
Echinacea pallida	Pale purple coneflower	4-inch purple daisies on 3-foot stalks
Echinacea purpurea	Purple coneflower	Prairie-forest edge; 6-inch pink, purple, or white daisies with orange centers

North American prairie native Culver's root (Veronicastrum virginicum) thrives throughout the Midwest.

PLANTS OF NORTHERN PRAIRIES, HUMID REGIONS (continued)

Latin Name	Common Name	Description
Eryngium yuccifolium	Rattlesnake-master	Yuccalike leaves
Filipendula rubra	Queen-of-the-prairie	Fragrant 6-foot herb with pink, cotton-candy-like flowers
Gentiana andrewsii	Bottle gentian	Clusters of 2-inch purple bottles on 2-foot stems in fall
Gentiana puberula	Downy gentian	Open, upright, 5-pointed purple chalices in late fall; very choice
Ipomoea leptophylla	Bush morning glory	Pink or purple 3-inch corolla; dry regions
Liatris aspera	Rough blazing star	5-foot spikes of purple blooms in late summer or early fall
Liatris cylindracea	Cylindric blazing star	3-foot spikes of lavender flowers; dry sites only
Liatris pycnostachya	Prairie blazing star	5-foot plants bearing showy purple flower clusters
Lithospermum canescens	Prairie puccoon	Clear orange fiddleheads on 1½ foot stems; very beautiful
Lobelia cardinalis	Cardinal flower	Bright scarlet flowers on 5-foot stems; wet areas
Parthenium integrifolium	Wild quinine	To 4 feet; clusters of white flowers; used in dried arrangements
Penstemon digitalis	White-flowered penstemon	Floriferous; 4-foot-tall; white flowers
Petalostemon candidum	White prairie clover	To 3 feet; white flowers; dry sites
Petalostemon purpureum	Purple prairie clover	To 3 feet; purple flowers; average moisture to dry sites
Phlox pilosa	Prairie phlox	2-foot clumps of bright pink flowers in spring
Physostegia virginiana	False dragonhead	Spreading plant with pink snapdragonlike blooms
Polytaenia nuttallii	Prairie parsley	Dry sites only; white seeds are held on plants and provide late-fall texture
Potentilla arguta	Prairie cinquefoil	Modest white flowers and showy rust seed heads; used in dried arrangements
Ratibida pinnata	Yellow coneflower	Very floriferous yellow daisy with drooping petals; one of best for bouquets
Rudbeckia subtomentosa	Sweet coneflower	Tall yellow daisy to 6 feet; floriferous and aromatic
Silphium laciniatum	Compass plant	A symbol of the prairie; to 14 feet; large yellow sunflowers on erect stems
Silphium terebinthinaceum	Prairie dock	Tall stems bearing clusters of small yellow daisies; basal elephant-ear leaves
Solidago rigida	Stiff goldenrod	Sulfur-yellow, flat-topped flower clusters turn to fluffy white in seed; easy to establish
Solidago speciosa	Showy goldenrod	4-foot golden plumes on wine-colored stems in late autumn; forms clumps
Veronicastrum virginicum	Culver's root	To 6 feet; clusters of white spikes at top of plant in late summer
Zizia aptera	Heart-leaved golden Alexander	Short spring bloomer with waxy, showy leaves and yellow flower clusters
Zizia aurea	Golden Alexander	To 3 feet; partial to moist sites; showy yellow flowers and dark green leaves

PONDS AND POND MAKING

A POOL TO ATTRACT WILDLIFE

Pebble beach
Gentle slope lets animals approach water gradually

Floating plants
Shade water and provide landing pads for insects

Rock basking places
Attract butterflies to warm themselves

Trees and shrubs
Attract beneficial insects and provide wildlife food and cover

Food for waterfowl
Includes duckweed and duck potato

Grasses
Provide cover near water year-round

Rock nooks and crannies
Give amphibians cool spots in summer and hibernation spots in winter

Wildlife-attracting marginal and bog plants
Provide food and nectar for a wide variety of animals

Ponds, marshes, and bogs are communities rich in plants and wildlife. Water is essential for all forms of plant and animal life. A pond in your garden will attract a variety of interesting wildlife both in and out of the water. A pond surrounded by wetland plants will provide an opportunity for a new and exciting realm of gardening.

Water is a host to all kinds of wildlife.

WATER IS NEEDED BY ALL WILDLIFE

Birds, mammals, amphibians, reptiles, and insects are all attracted to bodies of water, small or large. A garden with abundant food such as berries and dry-seed fruits and fresh water will abound with wildlife.

Water plants are easy to grow and very rewarding, with spectacular blooms and unusual foliage. Because they are often exotic, they draw comment and attract attention far more than do other garden plants.

Many beautiful native plants can be grown in an aquatic setting, as can a variety of exotics. Giant lotus and stunning water lilies are only a few of the exotic plants you can grow in and around your pond. Giant lotus are not natives but will completely adapt in many gardens. Adaptation usually depends on a plant's frost hardiness. Keep in mind that many plants that can adapt to climates warmer than their native home are less likely to tolerate colder winters.

Although delicate looking, water lilies like this are actually easy to grow.

On the pages that follow, you will find suggestions of aquatic plants for growing in the pond, as well as trees, shrubs, and perennials to plant nearby. Choose plants that suit your region.

TREES AND SHRUBS FOR MOIST AREAS NEAR THE POND

Your selection of plants will be broader if you locate the pond in full sun. Place trees on the north and east sides of the pond so the plants will be exposed to the full south and west sun. Use small trees, shrubs, and perennials to set off the pond and to provide a home for wildlife attracted by the water.

Avoid trees with a strong affinity for water. Although weeping willow and poplar seem natural by a pond—in nature they grow along creek beds and ponds—they are voracious guzzlers; full-size trees consume thousands of gallons of water each day. The roots of these trees will seek out the moist areas around a pond and choke out other plants. In time they may even damage the pond. The trees and shrubs listed here are well-behaved plants suitable for a pond environment, and their leaves are nontoxic to aquatic life.

Perhaps surprisingly, these waterside plants appreciate regular irrigation. Since ponds lined with plastic do not moisten the soil around them, in dry climates install drip irrigation. Design the system so that plants preferring marshy conditions are on different valves from plants preferring less water.

PLANTS FOR MARGINS OF THE POND

Many marsh and bog plants have interesting foliage or flowers. Several of these will grow in the shallow water at the edge of the pond. Others will grow around the perimeter but will need regular watering. Bog plants prefer heavy loam with some sand mixed in.

PLANTS FOR THE POND ITSELF

Aquatic plants root underwater and float to the surface. These plants generally require water more than a foot deep, and sometimes more than 2 feet deep. Aquatics include some of the most beautiful flowering plants. Indeed, water lilies have been so beloved that gardeners have built ponds just to grow them. Garden ponds are still often called lily ponds.

Water lilies grow freely throughout North America and most of the rest of the world. They are hardy and easy to grow. The hardiest of them will thrive in the far north, where ponds freeze into solid blocks of ice. Other types are adapted throughout the continent, including some outstanding subtropicals. Water lilies have large and aggressive roots and will spread quickly if not planted in containers.

Lotus are related to water lilies. They have showy flowers as large as 10 inches across and leaves as much as 3 feet across. Plant them in large containers about 3 feet square and place them so that the soil level in the container is about 6 inches below the surface of the water. Give them lots of room in the center of the pond—at least 50 square feet of water surface for one of the larger types. Dwarf types that take less room are available from some specialty growers.

When planting aquatics in containers, use rich, heavy loam mixed with 25 percent sand. Place a 3-inch layer of soil in the bottom of the container. Mix it thoroughly with a well-balanced, time-released granular fertilizer—1 cup of fertilizer for every 8 quarts of soil. Fill the rest of the container with soil that does not contain fertilizer. Add an inch of clean gravel on top to reduce the amount of soil mixing with the water.

If you have a special fondness for aquatic plants, consider building a series of ponds. Some could be shallow and some deep; especially suited to certain plant species or specific types of fish.

Purple irises and magenta primroses find conditions to their liking in the rich, wet soil of a backyard bog garden.

Ponds add more than beauty and wildlife. They also add a new realm of gardening with aquatic animals and plants.

MAKING A NATURAL POND

Whether your garden is in a prairie, a desert, or a woodland, your natural pond will be at home: Bodies of water are found in all environments. Some natural ponds are created by high water tables, some are fed by springs, and others are simply deep spots in a gurgling stream. They form their own microclimate— their own unique community—wherever they are.

In nature, most ponds accumulate silt and gradually fill in. This action is aided by eutrophication, a process associated with plant growth, particularly that of algae. As plant material dies, it forms sediment, which sinks to the bottom and gradually fills in the pond. Eutrophication is accelerated by the erosion of fertilizer and topsoil from surrounding fields and yards. To some extent this process will take place in your pond.

Wetlands support a great variety of plant life. Ponds in marshy areas support the widest variety. Plants on the edge of the pond live a dual life, standing in the water during wet seasons and on dry ground or in moist soil when the water is low. Some species of iris are particularly suited to a water garden. The most common and widespread is blue flag (*Iris versicolor*). For mild southern climates, select red iris (*Iris fulva*), a spectacular species from Louisiana with bronze-red flowers.

Families with young children must consider the hazards of a garden pond. Even shallow water can be dangerous, especially for infants and toddlers. It would be wise to postpone building a ground-level pool until children are older and can understand the hazards of water and can safely play near it.

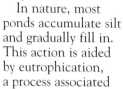

In a white cedar bog of South Carolina, tall yellow pitcher plants nod over floating Arum leaves.

A pond with a variety of depths can support many different plants. Here, two shallow-water marginals, blue rabbit's-ear iris and red 'Fireglow' Griffith's spurge, thrive near water lilies, which need water at least a foot or more deep.

NATURALISTIC DESIGN

This informal water feature, full of curves and turns, is a natural for a wooded lot and a casual, nature-oriented lifestyle.

A pond can be any shape and size that fits your yard and suits your inclinations. Ponds in nature are usually irregular in form and often irregular in depth. You could make your pond long and skinny or short and wide, a single pond or a group, on one level or in a series cascading down a hillside.

Consider two or more ponds of different depths for different types of wildlife and plants. Some animals are not compatible with others. For example, bass and some other game fish will eat tadpoles and goldfish. Think through your wishes and consider nature's requirements before you start digging.

Design your pond to fit existing contours, or regrade your yard to please your eye. Locate the pond on undisturbed, firm soil. This is important regardless of the material you use to line the pond, because settling can separate a clay liner, crack a concrete liner, or cause a flexible membrane liner to develop severe wrinkles. Because the water surface is always level, if a rigid liner tips even slightly, it will show. Severe settling will allow the pond water to spill out of its liner.

Common goldfish thrive in a garden pond. While not as exotic as larger koi, they are colorful and hardy. They also eat their share of mosquito larvae and other insects.

BUILDING A GARDEN POND

Varying pond depth allows for a greater variety of plant life. Water lilies here grow in 1½ feet of water, while plants at left rest on a shallow ledge.

Building a garden pond or other water feature is not difficult—even for beginners. You can read the instructions presented in this chapter and proceed with confidence, no matter what style water feature you have chosen. If you have a few basic home gardening tools, you're already well armed for the work. With two exceptions—electrical work and excavation of large projects—you probably won't have to hire an outside contractor.

Before beginning your pond, talk to a local building inspector. In some communities, permits are required for pools, although small garden pools may be exempt. The regulations may mandate a wall or fence if a garden pool exceeds a certain depth—18 inches in many communities.

Your pond should have shallow as well as deep areas to accommodate the needs of wildlife and aquatic plants. Shallow water attracts birds, many of which will bathe there. The shallows should extend onto a muddy beach; swallows and other birds and insects will use the mud for nests. Butterflies will drink in the shallows, and frogs will use them to climb out of the pond (otherwise they will drown).

Many mammals appreciate shallow water because it's easy for them to drink there. Some animals, such as raccoons, will use the shallows to wash their food before they eat.

Because algae thrive in the light and warmth of shallow water, your pond should have a range of depths. Besides, many aquatic plants have specific depth requirements. Lotus and large water lilies, for instance, need deep water. Dig the pond so that its finished depth will be at least 2 feet in the areas intended for

WATER DEPTHS

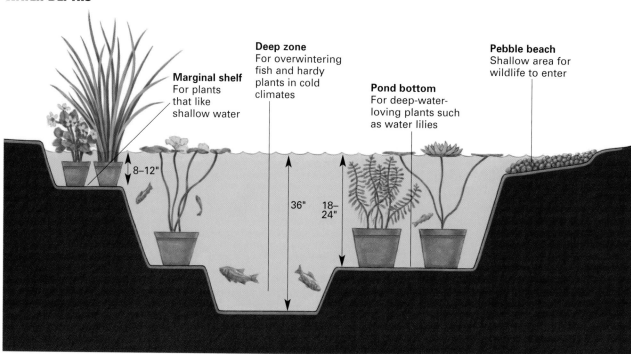

Marginal shelf
For plants that like shallow water

8–12"

Deep zone
For overwintering fish and hardy plants in cold climates

36"   18–24"

Pond bottom
For deep-water-loving plants such as water lilies

Pebble beach
Shallow area for wildlife to enter

Natural edging stones are incorporated here to soften the linear edging formed from the pond's concrete lining.

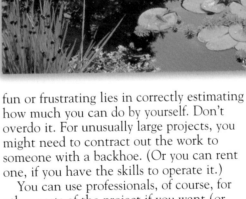

This small waterfall helps aerate the water for fish. However, it doesn't disturb the surface so much that water lilies—which love still water— can't thrive.

these large plants. Fish prefer deep water, too—at least 2 feet—for the coolness and for protection from predators.

Installing underwater features such as logs, stones, and ledges provides additional shelter for aquatic wildlife and increases visual interest in the pond.

Moving water adds sound as well as visual interest. A bubbling stream, a small waterfall, or a small stream of water from a piece of split bamboo are easy features to add to a pond; they can provide a feast for the eyes and music for the ears.

To create moving water, install a small submersible pump in the lowest spot in your pond. Use flexible plastic pipe to transport the water to the top of your waterfall or the highest end of your stream. Screen the pump inlet to protect it and prevent fish from entering it.

Electrical work and excavation will be the most daunting parts of the project. Although it is advisable for safety's sake—and may be required by city building code—to hire out most electrical work to a licensed electrician and to contract large-scale excavations, you still need to educate yourself on the basics. Then you'll be able talk more knowledgeably with the contractor, if you hire one.

Excavating even a small installation can be a chore—or it can remind you of the days when you were 12 years old and digging a big hole was pure fun. The key to whether it is

fun or frustrating lies in correctly estimating how much you can do by yourself. Don't overdo it. For unusually large projects, you might need to contract out the work to someone with a backhoe. (Or you can rent one, if you have the skills to operate it.)

You can use professionals, of course, for other parts of the project if you want (or absolutely have to). However, you'll spend more and miss out on the fun of building your own water feature.

Garden pool installation, like most home improvement projects, is easier to accomplish with two people. Whether you're installing flexible liner, leveling a rigid liner, laying stone, hauling away dirt, or just in need of a second opinion, a helper greatly speeds up the project.

And, as you launch into building your garden pond, allow yourself plenty of time for each step. Most homeowners tend to be overly optimistic with their estimates of the time it will take to complete a project. Remember that there are always unexpected complications, unforeseen trips to the hardware store, and many other time-consuming tasks you won't anticipate.

BUILDING A GARDEN POND
continued

DIGGING IN

Start by marking the site with a garden hose, rope, or garden lime. Then fine-tune the outline with stakes (every foot or so) and twine. Cut along the outline with a spade; then remove the top layer of sod. If you're going to use turf as edging, cut the sod approximately 4 inches in from the outline of the pond. Remove the sod inside the outline and peel back the 4-inch strip. After installing the liner, flip the sod back over it.

To edge with stones or other material, dig an outwardly sloping shelf (6 to 8 inches wide by 2 inches deep) for the liner and the edging. The trench should be deep enough for the edging stones to sit flush with the ground or 3 to 4 inches deep for a concrete footing for edges that will get heavy traffic.

With the sod removed, mark the outlines for marginal shelves; then begin digging from the center outward. Dig 2 inches deeper than the pool depth to allow for sand underlayment (less for other materials). As you dig, angle the sides outward slightly, about 20 degrees.

DIGGING A POOL

1. Mark the outline of the pond with a garden hose, rope, or line of flour, fine soil, or garden lime. Live with the outline for a week or so to discover how well the new feature fits into the landscape and how it will affect traffic patterns.

2. Remove turf. Use it to fill bare spots in the lawn or set it aside in a pile of its own to compost. If you have a large quantity, use it as the base of a berm or a raised bed. Stack it in the spot for the berm; then cover with several inches of topsoil.

3. As you dig, keep the pond edge level. If it is not level, the liner will show. Check by resting a carpenters level on a straight board laid across the pond. Work all around the pond, checking every shelf and side of the pool so that there are no surprises.

4. Create a spot to overwinter plants and fish. In cold areas, you'll need a zone in the pool that won't freeze. It should be up to 3 feet deep and as wide as it is deep. Be sure this deep zone isn't in the same spot you want to place a pump or fountain.

5. Dig the shelf for the marginal plants about 8 to 12 inches deep. Position the marginal-plant shelf so that the plants frame your view of the water garden. Then dig a ledge for the edging as deep as the edging material and slightly less wide.

6. Toss the soil into a wheelbarrow or onto a tarp to protect your lawn. If it is in good condition, use it to fill in other spots in the landscape or to build a slope for a waterfall. Or haul it to a construction site that needs fill dirt.

Make sure the edges of the pond are level or the liner will show. With a small project, place a carpenter's level on a straight piece of 2×4, checking all around the pond. For a large project, put a stake in the center of the pond with its top at the planned water level. Rest one end of a long straight board on the stake and the other end on the edge of the pool. Check the level. Rotate the board a few feet, again noting the level. Repeat until you return to the starting point.

Use the removed sod to patch bare spots in the yard or add it to a compost pile. If the topsoil is in reasonably good condition, add it to the vegetable garden, spread it on flower beds, or create new beds and berms. If you're installing a rigid liner, set aside the soil to backfill around the liner. Put the soil in a wheelbarrow or on a large tarp or piece of plastic to protect the lawn. Discard clay-laden subsoil or use it to build up a slope for a waterfall. Dump larger amounts at a landfill.

ELECTRICITY AND WATER SUPPLY

If you are planning a moving water feature, the selection of a site for the pond depends in part on how you will get electricity to it. Fountains and waterfalls use an electrical pump, operating on normal household current, to suck up and recirculate the pond water. It is easiest to use an electrical outlet on the outside of the house or one that is accessible through a garage or basement window. For aesthetics' sake, the electric cable—be sure it is designed for outdoor use—leading from the outlet to the pump can be buried under soil or covered by stones. If the pond site is some distance from your house, you can bury a long cable inside a conduit, but it will require a fair bit of excavation.

You may also want to install underground water pipes and a spigot near the pool. You will need water not only for the initial filling of the pool but also for topping up the water as it evaporates. In summer, evaporation can be quite rapid; the water level can fall as much as half an inch per day. For the health of plants and fish, as well as the appearance of the pool, you will need to add water to the pool at least once a week during hot, dry summers. You can fill a garden pool of any size from a garden hose—no permanent water supply is needed. However, if the pool is some distance from the house, you may find it more convenient to have a spigot near the pool. Also consider automated filling devices. Several varieties are available at irrigation supply stores.

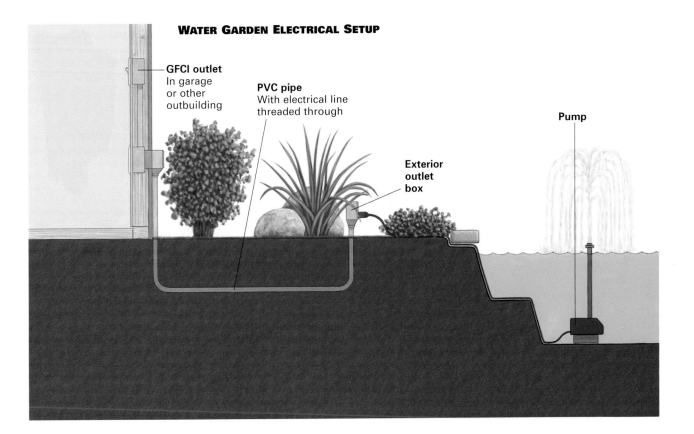

WATER GARDEN ELECTRICAL SETUP

GFCI outlet
In garage or other outbuilding

PVC pipe
With electrical line threaded through

Exterior outlet box

Pump

INSTALLING A FLEXIBLE LINER

Flexible liner has become popular largely because it is easy to install. However, you must install it properly to prevent the liner from showing (which speeds deterioration) and leaks from developing.

LINER: After digging and ensuring that the edges of the pond are level, remove any rough items—roots, rocks, debris, buried shards of glass—anything that might puncture the lining. Spread out the liner in the sun for an hour or two to let it soften, which makes it much easier to work with.

If you need to seam two pieces, do it now, using solvent cement or adhesive designed especially for this purpose.

Avoid dragging the liner over the ground or rocks and gravel; this may cause rips or punctures in the liner.

UNDERLAYMENT: This layer cushions the liner, adding to its life and preventing rocks and twigs from puncturing it. Use a layer of damp sand, old carpet, or underlayment made specifically for use with flexible liner. The layer should be one half to 2 inches thick.

Installing a flexible liner is fairly simple. Although one person can accomplish the job, it goes faster with two.

Edged with stones and supporting plants, a pond lined with flexible liner appears natural.

Cover the sides and the bottom of the pool with the underlayment. Many lining materials are easier to work with if you wet them first, especially when applying them up the sides of the pool. Also, cut triangles in the fabric materials to fit the contours of the pond.

SPREADING THE FABRIC: Depending on the size of your garden pond, spreading the liner may take one or several people. Try flapping it like a sheet (up and down) to force air under the liner and help it float into place. As much as possible, smooth out the liner and fold it neatly to fit into the contours and corners of the pond. Don't stretch the liner.

Leave a little wrinkle of extra liner in the bottom of the pond—"pinch an inch" here and there. This allows the liner to spread a little when the soil settles and is particularly wise in earthquake-prone areas. Leave as much excess liner as possible (at least 6 inches) over the outside edge of the pool. Use bricks or stones to hold it in place temporarily.

ADDING WATER: Fill the pool with a few inches of water; then readjust the liner, once again pleating, folding, or arranging it to get as smooth a fit as possible. Move the bricks if needed. Fill the pond about halfway and adjust the liner and bricks again. Folds and wrinkles will always occur. Once adjustments are made, fill the pond almost completely.

Trim the liner with heavy scissors or a utility knife, leaving enough excess to protect the edging shelf. Cover the edging liner with soil (or concrete if the edge around the pond must support heavy traffic or a heavy edging material). Then you can install the edging, such as stones, letting it overhang the pond by at least 2 to 3 inches.

EDGING TIP

Here's a good way to prevent the liner from showing. Dig the edging shelf deep enough for a double layer of flagstones, cut stones, bricks, or other edging. Lay the first layer of edging; then wrap the liner over the first layer as shown and top with the second. Water can now be filled to the middle of the first layer of edging. With one layer of edging, the water can be filled only a little below the bottom of the edging.

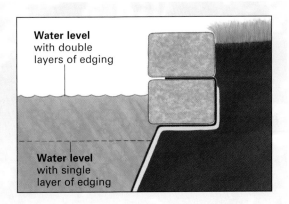

Water level with double layers of edging

Water level with single layer of edging

INSTALLING THE LINER STEP-BY-STEP

1. CUSHION THE HOLE WITH UNDERLAYMENT. This can be moist sand, old carpet, or underlayment made for water gardens. Cover both the bottom and the sides. Laying underlayment can be frustrating; cut triangles at corners and curves to help fit contours.

2. POSITION LINER. Let the liner warm in the sun for at least an hour to soften. Drape it loosely in the hole, arranging and pleating as needed. (This may be a job for two or more people.) Anchor the sides with bricks or stones, taking care to not stretch the liner.

3. ADJUST THE LINER. Add a few inches of water to the pool to settle the liner. Pleat and tuck the liner, as necessary, to make it fit the contours and corners of the water feature.

4. PREPARE FOR EDGING. Fill the pond with a few more inches of water. Adjust liner; then fill to just below the edging shelf. Trim the liner.

5. INSTALL EDGING. This can be flagstone, brick, cut stone, or other edging. Do a final trim of the liner. You can pat a little soil in behind the edging to conceal any visible liner.

INSTALLING A RIGID, PREFORMED POND LINER

Although a rigid liner is a little more difficult to install than a flexible liner, it is still relatively simple. The key is ensuring the liner is level at all times.

Start by putting the liner in position before you begin to dig. You may need to use bricks to hold up portions of the liner if it has varying depths. Level the liner as much as possible. Then pound stakes every foot or so around the liner, following the contour of its lip. Further mark around it with rope, a garden hose, flour, or garden lime. Then dig the hole to conform to the shape of the liner, measuring frequently to check depths and widths. The hole needs to be larger than the liner—allow an extra 2 inches around its perimeter and 2 to 3 inches at the bottom.

Remove any rocks or sharp objects as you work. Set the liner in place to see if it fits, and make adjustments as needed. Remove the liner and fill the bottom of the hole with a combination of sand and fine soil. Level this mix with a short board (called a screed), then firmly tamp the soil to create a stable base. Make sure the bottom, marginal shelves, and edges are still absolutely level in all directions after tamping. For large ponds, set the level on a straight piece of lumber.

Again, place the liner in the hole, pressing it down gently so that it fits snugly in the deepest areas. Recheck for level. You may need to remove the liner several times to make adjustments.

Once the pond is perfectly level, fill the bottom with 4 inches of water to stabilize it. Then begin backfilling around the sides of the pond with a mixture of sand and fine soil, checking for level as you go. Gently tamp the soil-sand mixture in with a shovel handle or the end of a 2×4. Be certain to fill all voids

INSTALLING A PREFORMED LINER

1. Position the liner where you plan to locate the pond, using bricks if necessary to keep it level. Then pound stakes in place around the liner and use them as a guide to mark the exact outline. If the pool is small, make a template by tracing around the lip on cardboard instead.

2. Dig out the shape of the liner, making it 2 inches wider and 2 to 3 inches deeper than the actual liner. Conform your digging to the shape of shelves and deep zones, measuring depth, width, and level frequently.
    Monitor your work by lowering the liner into place and making adjustments.

3. Once the hole is dug, make sure there aren't any sharp objects or stones left on the bottom. Then fill the bottom with moist sand, fine soil, or a combination of the two. Use a short board to level the bottom. Tamp it down firmly and check the level once again.

and pockets, especially around and under the marginal shelves.

Fill the pond with another 4 inches of water. Never allow the water level to be higher than the backfill or the liner will bulge outward. Add more backfill then 4 more inches of water. Repeat until you have completed the backfilling and the pond is full.

If the liner has a flat lip, work a foundation of crushed stone topped with damp sand under the lip and around liner edges. Then position the stone or other finish edging on top of the liner edge.

If the lip is concave or otherwise can't hold the weight of the edging (or heavy traffic), dig and pour a 3- to 4-inch-deep concrete footing that extends beyond and over the top of the lip. Embed the edging in the concrete, overhanging the inside of the liner by 1 to 2 inches. The weight of the edging will be

Surrounded by blooming flowers and bordered by stones, a pond is usually the central attraction of the garden.

supported by the concrete foundation.

After mortar between the stones has cured (about a week), scrub with muriatic acid to neutralize the lime. Drain the pond (runoff from the acid will make the water toxic), rinse, and refill.

4. Lower the liner into place, checking the level. You may need to remove the liner several times to make adjustments.

5. Add 4 inches of water and begin backfilling. Tamp the soil with a shovel handle or a 2×4 as you work. Backfill again and add 4 more inches of water, keeping the water level lower than the backfill. Repeat until filled.

Although preformed liners are ideal for formal gardens, they also can be made to look very natural. This one, surrounded by stone, has a small stream flowing into it.

POND CARE

The plants and animals you place in your pond will be joined by others placed there by nature as your pond seeks a natural ecological balance. In the first few weeks of a pond's life, the liner and the clean stones you placed in it will become coated with a layer of shiny, rippling green. This is filamentous algae, which, in fact, will also turn the water green. If the water is deep enough (18 to 24 inches), this will clear as the life in the pond finds its own balance.

If you filled your pond with water from a municipal or private water authority, the water was probably chlorinated. Chlorine evaporates into the atmosphere as harmless gas within 24 hours, so tap water will usually not harm fish and plants.

Some municipalities and other water authorities use chlorine compounds that leave a residue harmful to plants and fish. Check with your water supplier to determine if they use chloramine or chlorine dioxide. These compounds will not dissipate into the air in a few hours; however, pet stores and aquarium retailers sell products to neutralize these compounds. Use them when you fill the pond or when you top it off.

A natural pond in your garden requires little maintenance. Snip faded flowers from the water lilies or lotus and remove dying leaves. Remove fallen tree leaves with a net to prevent excess decaying organic material. Top off the pond with water once a week during warm weather.

Fall colors are lovely around a garden pool. Be sure to skim fallen leaves from the pond daily to avoid problems.

Aquatic plants are moderately heavy feeders. Flowering types such as waterlilies and lotus should be fed as the flower buds are forming. Feed them with slow-dissolving fertilizer tablets by scraping back the gravel over the soil around the roots and inserting from one to four tablets into the soil around the plant. Place the tablets at least 2 inches into the soil so that the plants, not the pond, will receive the benefit of the fertilizer. Replace the layer of gravel. Use this method for all container plants in water gardens and bogs.

Cleaning a pond is a chore you'll need to perform only once in a while, but it can help keep a pond in balance. Cleaning reduces certain kinds of algae and other pond problems.

PLANTS OF WATER GARDENS

Latin Name	Common Name	Description
TREES		
Acer grandidentatum	Bigtooth maple	Rockies and Southwest
Acer macrophyllum	Big-leaf maple	Pacific Coast; to 100 feet
Alnus species	Alder	About 30 species (vary across U.S.); moist soils, cool climates
Nyssa sylvatica	Black gum	Eastern U.S.; fall color; to 100 feet
Platanus species	Sycamore	*P. occidentalis* in East; *P. racemosa* in California; *P. wrightii* in Arizona and New Mexico
Populus species	Poplar	30–40 species (vary across U.S.); easy to cultivate
Taxodium distichum	Bald cypress	Eastern U.S.; can also grow submerged in water
Umbellularia californica	California laurel	Pacific Coast; large tree with aromatic foliage
SHRUBS		
Calycanthus floridus	Carolina allspice	Southern U.S.; to 10 feet
Clethra alnifolia	Sweet pepperbush	Eastern U.S.; very fragrant white to pink flowers; form clumps
Cornus stolonifera	Red osier dogwood	Transcontinental; easy cultivation
Ilex glabra	Inkberry	Eastern U.S.; evergreen holly with black fruits
Myrica species	Wax myrtle	Eastern U.S. and Pacific Coast evergreen shrub
Prunus virginiana	Western chokecherry	Fruit used in jellies
Viburnum trilobum	Highbush cranberry	Bright red berries
ANNUALS AND PERENNIALS		
Asclepias incarnata	Swamp milkweed	Showy pink flowers
Eupatorium maculatum	Joe-Pye weed	Showy purple flowers
Helenium autumnale	Sneezeweed	Yellow flowers; to 5 feet
Mimulus species	Monkey flower	Primarily in western U.S.; most species are showy
Monarda didyma	Scarlet bee balm	Eastern U.S.; very showy
Symplocarpus foetidus	Skunk cabbage	Strangely beautiful; purple and green foliage
SEMIAQUATICS (Grow near water, or with their roots occasionally in shallow water)		
Acorus calamus	Sweet flag	Transcontinental; aromatic; to 6 feet
Asclepias incarnata	Swamp milkweed	Pink showy flowers
Betula lutea	Yellow birch	Eastern species; brown peeling bark
Calamagrostis canadensis	Bluejoint grass	To 6 feet; pink inflorescences
Caltha palustris	Marsh marigold	Flowers like giant golden buttercups
Cephalanthus occidentalis	Buttonbush	Handsome shrub; transcontinental
Chelone glabra	Turtlehead	White flowers; host plant for Baltimore butterfly
Iris versicolor	Wild blue flag	Eastern U.S.; stems to 3 feet
Lobelia cardinalis	Cardinal flower	Brilliant scarlet flowers; transcontinental
Lobelia siphilitica	Great blue lobelia	Eastern U.S.; to 3 feet
Phragmites communis	Wild reed	To 8 feet; transcontinental
Physostegia virginiana	False dragonhead	Pink flowers; eastern U.S.
Typha species	Cattail	Transcontinental; about 15 species
AQUATICS		
Nelumbo lutea	American lotus	Giant peltate leaves; seedpods used in dried arrangements
Nuphar species	Yellow pond lily	Water lily; transcontinental
Nymphaea tuberosa	White water lily	Flowers showy; tubers and seeds are prime duck foods
Peltandra virginica	Arrow arum	Also called duck corn, referring to the greenish black fruit at base of the spadix
Pontederia cordata	Pickerel weed	Very handsome arrow-shaped leaves and purple flowers
Sagittaria species	Arrowhead	Arrow-shaped leaves; prime duck food
Sparganium eurycarpum	Giant bur weed	Spherical fruit bear corn-sized seeds that are food for waterfowl

Cardinal flower's bright red spires bloom over dark toothy foliage.

Native marsh marigold (Caltha palustris) clings to a water-washed stream bank.

PLANTS & PLANTING

Before you head for a garden center, do a little homework. Know your eco-region and its cold-hardiness zone, as indicated by the maps on pages 17 and 92. Also review the growing conditions in your yard—areas vary. Is the soil in the beds well- or poorly drained? Fertile or lean? Does it steadily retain moisture or dry out between waterings? Will your plants get full sun or partial shade? How do the sun and shade patterns change with the seasons? Are some spots windier than others? What microclimates exist in your yard that may permit you to grow plants unique to that small niche?

Take notes to have handy while mulling over plant choices and shopping. This information is vital to the future well-being of your garden. When matched to the site, your plants will be

Discover new and unusual regional plants for the garden at local plant sales or a swap sponsored by an arboretum or plant society.

Take steps to protect your new tree on the way home or your investment may be ruined. Securely wrapping the tree helps reduce dehydration caused by wind and protects the leaves from shredding or tattering.

Mail-order plants usually arrive dormant with bare roots enclosed in sphagnum moss and wrapped in plastic (above) or as potted plants with the top growth visible.

Balled-and-burlapped trees, their trunks wrapped for protection, are a common sight at nurseries. Getting them home safe and sound and in good health is the real trick.

healthy, bloom readily, and stand a better chance of fending off insects and disease. Then peruse the lists of recommended plants that will please you and will happily—and healthfully— grow in your yard.

Finally, think about where you'll find plants. Your phone book can direct you to local garden centers. Mail-order sources can be reached by phone or the Internet. Here's an overview of each source as well as pros and cons.

GARDEN CENTERS

Buying at garden centers lets you see exactly what you're getting, carry out your purchases, and plant them right away. Experts there can help you fine-tune your shopping list and answer questions about plants in stock that you may not have researched. The plants may carry a guarantee, and the garden center's location may make replacement convenient. In general, plants at garden centers are available in 4-inch pots or 1-, 2-, or 5-gallon containers. Some offer smaller or larger sizes. Garden centers tend to stock only several hundred of the tens of thousands of existing species and varieties. Relying solely on a local garden center means you may need to make substitutions for the original choices on your list.

MAIL ORDER

Mail order lets you shop without pulling out of the driveway. But the real enticement is being able to track down specific varieties not available at local garden centers, as well as having a choice of size and price.

To get started, review a few garden catalogs (you can find their advertisments in any gardening magazine). Or, with a couple of keystrokes, put the Internet to work. Enter a specific plant name in a search engine. You'll turn up dozens of online catalogs offering that plant.

Remember, with mail-order sources, you won't be able to inspect plants close up. A catalog might indicate plant size, but quality may be unknown. It's wise to limit your first order until you're acquainted with the quality and size of plants sent by a particular retailer.

Mail-order selections usually arrive potted or bare-root (dormant, with roots protected in a moist medium). It is also possible to find perennials as first-year seedlings packed in plastic cells, typically six to a pack. Perennials in six-packs cost much less than container-grown plants. If you buy plants this small, however, you may have to wait an extra year for a strong garden display. Try to plant your order as soon as possible. If you must wait a few days, keep plants moist and cool. Do not store them longer than a week.

IMPROVING SOIL

Any soil can be made loose, well-drained, and weed free. However, for the best combination of these traits, plus fertility and moisture retention, the ideal is loam.

Loam is a mix of sand, silt, and clay. It has enough tiny particles (20 percent) to be fertile, enough large sand particles (40 percent) to drain quickly and warm up early in spring, and enough medium-size silt particles (40 percent) to unite the clay and sand in loose, round crumbs. When topsoil is needed to build up existing soil, it is best to bring in a loam.

If your soil has an excess of one particle type, it can cause problems. For example, excess clay makes for a sticky soil that clumps, preventing water and nutrients from passing through. Overly sandy soil is unable to retain moisture or nutrients. In such situations, gardeners often focus on changing the texture of the soil (relative amounts of sand, silt, and clay). But improving the structure (the way individual soil particles bind together) is a better way to improve plant growth and is much easier to change than texture.

Well-structured soil breaks apart into small granules. It holds water, air, and nutrients better than poorly structured soil, which collapses into disconnected grains when wet.

To improve soil structure, add organic matter at every opportunity. Microorganisms feed on the organic matter and produce a "glue" that coats mineral particles and causes them to hold together in moisture-, air-, and nutrient-retaining crumbs.

Till or turn organic matter into the soil as you prepare the bed or add it by sheet composting. Aim for a 2- to 3-inch layer of moistened peat or compost, or a 3- to 4-inch

Amend ground-cover and flower beds with organic matter and fertilizer before planting.

Clay soil (right) can be readily molded. Organic matter (above) loosens it up.

layer of tree leaves. Keep the organic matter content high by using an organic mulch and natural forms of fertilizers such as manure.

MAINTAINING GOOD SOIL: Routinely loosen soil by cultivating regularly with a hoe, minitiller, or fork. This is especially important in soils with a high percentage of silt because these tend to "cap"—the surface layer becomes dense and nearly impervious to air and water. Also spread a 1- to 3-inch blanket of organic matter on the soil surface as a mulch to encourage worms and soil microorganisms. Add amendments every time you rearrange, add, or divide plants.

PLANTING TREES AND SHRUBS

The best times of year to plant are midspring and early autumn. In southwestern deserts and mild winter regions of California, fall planting is by far preferred. Frost-tender plants are best planted in spring in all regions.

Overcast and drizzly days are ideal for planting. Avoid the middle of a hot day—when water from leaves is lost more quickly than it can be replaced. Even if no permanent damage is done, recovering from wilt consumes energy that the plant could have used to push roots into the new site.

If you must plant in the hot sun, erect shade screens. Plant into moist, friable soil and water each plant immediately afterward.

TREES: Plant trees first so you'll have room to maneuver without stepping on other plants. Dig holes twice as wide as root balls if space allows but only as deep as the root ball. The top of the root ball should be level with the surrounding soil. Digging holes too deep is a common mistake. As soil settles, so does the tree, and the roots may suffocate. If you dig your hole too deep, compact soil at the bottom of the hole to support the root ball.

Stand back (in the place from which you'll view the tree most often) and examine your tree after placing it in the hole. Rotate the plant until it presents its best face. For trees grown in containers with light, soil-less media, mix amendments with native soil to form a half-and-half mixture and fill the hole. For field-grown trees with a root ball of soil similar to that in your yard, avoid adding amendments. Water the soil periodically as you fill. Never tamp soil when planting; small air pockets are part of the soil structure and help transport water to roots. Form a moat of excess soil around the perimeter, mulch inside the ring, and fill the moat slowly with water several times; let it soak in completely. Water daily until new growth appears. In hot weather, new trees may need watering twice a day.

SHRUBS: To get your composition right, set your shrubs throughout the bed, while still in their containers, before planting the first one. This will minimize damage to roots. Follow the shape of both your front and rear bed lines. Fill middle sections, but don't form recognizable rows. The shrubs will grow together in a mass—forming a shape instead of a line. Space them no closer than two-thirds of their mature spread.

Shrub planting is very similar to tree planting. Dig holes wider than they are deep and make sure the root ball is level with or slightly higher than the surrounding soil. Mulch over the shrub roots, but keep the mulch away from the stem crown; it may cause rot. Use triangular spacing for setting shrubs, groundcovers, perennials, and annuals in beds. Mulch perennial beds well to form an extra winter blanket for roots and bulbs and to keep your beds looking neat. Most perennials should be dug and divided every few years to keep them from overcrowding.

TREE PLANTING

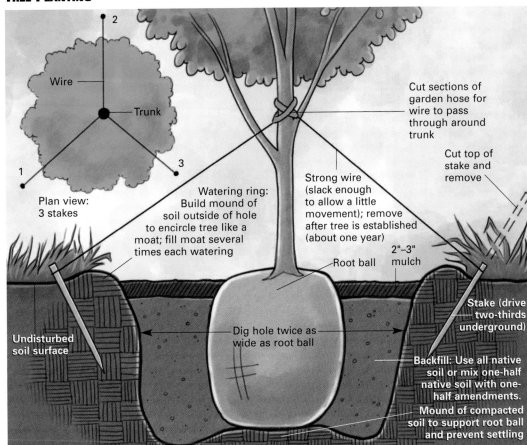

Wire

Trunk

1

2

3

Plan view: 3 stakes

Watering ring: Build mound of soil outside of hole to encircle tree like a moat; fill moat several times each watering

Cut sections of garden hose for wire to pass through around trunk

Cut top of stake and remove

Strong wire (slack enough to allow a little movement); remove after tree is established (about one year)

Root ball

2"–3" mulch

Stake (drive two-thirds underground)

Undisturbed soil surface

Dig hole twice as wide as root ball

Backfill: Use all native soil or mix one-half native soil with one-half amendments.

Mound of compacted soil to support root ball and prevent settling

PLANTING PERENNIALS AND TRANSPLANTING

Well-planted perennials thrive. They have room to grow, they are not planted too low or too high in the ground, and each one has a watering crater.

Perennials that have been in a dark package in the mail and those sold from inside a greenhouse in early spring are not ready to be planted outdoors. When buying perennials from an outdoor sales area, ask whether they have been hardened off or simply moved out each day from indoors. If the plants are fresh from a greenhouse, place them in a spot protected from the wind and midday sun for a few days. At night, cover them against rapid cooling or move them into a protected area—near the house or in a shed, for example. The next day, give the plants an additional hour of late-morning or mid-afternoon sun. Protect them again at night. Increase the light and expose them to wind over two more days before planting.

TRANSPLANTING FROM THE WILD

Transplanting wild plants into your garden is rarely appropriate. In many states, it is illegal to collect wild plants. Although often done in the past by avid gardeners, collecting plants in the wild has led some species almost to extinction. It is also difficult to move plants from their natural habitat to the garden successfully, and few survive for more than a season or two. And it is no longer necessary to find many native species in this way because they are now commercially grown in nurseries. Those species still unavailable from commercial sources can usually be propagated from seed or cuttings obtained from other gardeners.

The only acceptable occasion for digging plants from the wild is when the area is about to be leveled and developed. Be sure to obtain permission from the landowner in advance. If you can, prepare your garden areas for the wild plants before you dig them, learning everything possible of their habitat requirements, and providing soil pH, moisture, and light intensity to match their natural environment. Arrive with a shovel, twine, pails, and plastic bags or tarps, depending on the size of the plants. Remove the plants by digging carefully around each root ball, trying not to sever any roots, and gradually digging beneath the plant and lifting it from the earth. Take as large a root ball as possible and

SHRUB PLANTING

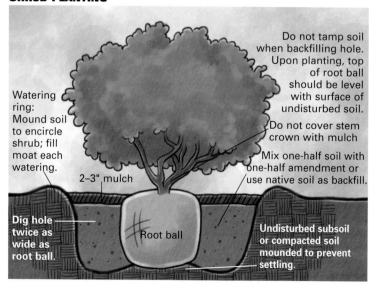

Watering ring: Mound soil to encircle shrub; fill moat each watering.

2–3" mulch

Dig hole twice as wide as root ball.

Root ball

Do not tamp soil when backfilling hole. Upon planting, top of root ball should be level with surface of undisturbed soil.

Do not cover stem crown with mulch

Mix one-half soil with one-half amendment or use native soil as backfill.

Undisturbed subsoil or compacted soil mounded to prevent settling.

Always handle plants by the sides of the root balls—never use the stem as a handle. Set plants in holes so the top of the root ball is level with adjacent soil surfaces. If the plant is lower, remove it and add backfill before resetting the plant.

Forming a moat around newly planted trees and shrubs only takes a little time but makes a big difference. The ring of soil surrounding the hole, not the root ball, helps contain water until it seeps down to roots.

When unpotting a perennial, spread your fingers around the stems to support the soil's weight. Invert the pot and lift it off with your other hand.

When roots are pot-bound, slice partly up into the root ball from the bottom and spread the roots wide across mounded soil in the bottom of the planting hole.

Check depth as you plant. The top of the root ball should be level or slightly higher than surrounding soil.

Plant bare-root perennials with their growth buds barely covered or within an inch of the surface. Make a mound of soil in the hole and spread the bare roots over it.

wrap it securely to avoid damage on the trip home. Once home, immediately set the plants in their permanent location. If you can't plant them immediately, set them all in a trench in a well-worked bed or pile of good soil, pull the soil over the root balls, and water them thoroughly. Move these plants as soon as possible to their permanent garden positions.

MANAGING GROWTH OF A NATURAL LANDSCAPE

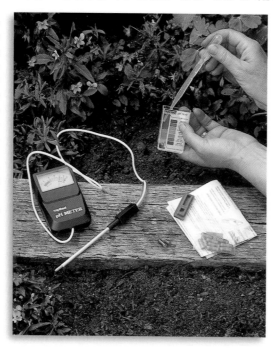

Soil test kits are available from garden centers and hardware stores. Knowing whether soil is acidic or alkaline will help you choose plants that will thrive in your garden. You can also add amendments to improve the pH as needed.

Mowing makes quick work of cleaning up a large bed of low-growing ground-covers. Raise mower blades to their highest setting.

You might assume that after planting a natural landscape, you're all done. After all, isn't letting nature take its course natural? Yes and no.

All gardening is ultimately about managing plant growth by pruning, fertilizing, watering, shearing, harvesting, protecting, and using a host of techniques to keep plants healthy and looking their best. Natural gardening takes this one step further; it uses subtle techniques

to encourage the growth of some plants and discourage others.

Many of these techniques are based on the concept of limiting factors. This concept states that the factors in shortest supply are those that limit growth. For example, if warm summer rainfall in the South has leached nitrogen and potassium from your soil, these minerals may be the primary limit to the growth of your plants. By adding these minerals to some parts of the garden and withholding them in others, you can control the growth of plants in these places.

In the arid West, water may be the limiting factor; selective watering can be the key to managing plant growth. In a wooded garden, light may be limiting. In such a case, growth can be managed by selectively thinning the tree canopy to allow more light to penetrate.

Here are some of the techniques used by natural gardeners that are not commonly practiced by most gardeners.

SELECTIVE FERTILIZING: Instead of fertilizing the entire garden at once, or giving all the plants all the fertilizer they can use, apply fertilizer selectively, to only those plants whose growth you wish to favor. In other areas of the garden, apply various nutrients for selective effects. Nitrogen is helpful everywhere. Phosphorous and potassium are helpful in areas with copious warm summer rain. Calcium is helpful where the soil is very acidic, sulfur where the soil is alkaline.

SELECTIVE WATERING: In the arid West, use a drip-irrigation system to water only those plants you wish to favor.

SELECTIVE THINNING: Favor plants growing under trees by thinning the tree canopy through selective pruning to allow more light to reach the ground.

SELECTIVE MOWING: Adapt your mowing schedule to the type of vegetation you have. Weekly mowing favors turfgrass. Many prairie plants, on the other hand, respond best to a late-summer mowing, which mimics the action of summer grass fires. Late mowing favors these plants and slows or stops the growth of trees and shrubs.

Even more subtle techniques can be used to enhance plant growth. For example, placing a large rock next to a plant in a crowded area favors its growth by reducing root competition in the area covered by the rock. The success of this technique can be seen by observing plants growing next to rocks and sidewalks; they are often more vigorous than those growing elsewhere.

WEEDING AND MULCHING

Trees with dense canopies, such as Southern magnolia, let little light pass through.

Limb up these trees to remove light-blocking lower branches. Light can then reach the ground from the side.

Thinning opens up the canopy so that light is able to filter through the branches to the ground.

Maintenance for groundcovers includes weeding, mulching, fertilizing, watering, pruning or mowing, and sometimes thinning.

Although individual plants may establish quickly, it takes time for the beds to fill in. For that reason, weeding is vital in the early years of a groundcover's life. Although you worked hard to eliminate weeds before planting, they will still pop up. Even well-established beds can become weedy. Vines, with their loose growth habits, are especially prone to letting weeds encroach.

If left unchecked, weeds can take over both new and well-filled-in beds. Check beds weekly, especially in the growing season, to catch weeds as they emerge. Then they can be simply hoed or pulled.

Weeds are easiest to pull, and displace the least soil as you pull them, when the soil is moist. So weed after watering or after a rain. Remove the entire plant, roots and all, by grasping it close to its base and pulling in an even motion. This helps prevent the weed's top from snapping off, leaving its roots to regrow. Wear gloves with rubber grips; they provide a better hold on the weed, as well as protect your hands.

To remove deeply rooted weeds, use a fish-tail weeder (also called an asparagus knife or dandelion fork). Slip the tool under the weed's roots; then pry the entire plant out of the ground. Remove pulled weeds from the bed so they can't reroot.

You can also control the weeds with herbicides, especially postemergence products. The trick to using herbicides effectively and safely in established beds is to select the right herbicide for your needs. Look for products that are specific to the weed problem and are safe to use on the groundcover. For example, a grass-specific herbicide, such as fluazifop, can be sprayed over broad-leaved ground-covers to control bermudagrass without harming the groundcover. An herbicide's label should clearly state which weeds it will control and which plants it can be used on.

Follow label directions explicitly and apply herbicides on still days so wind won't blow them onto ornamental plants. In some cases, you may be able to cover neighboring plants before applying herbicides to the weeds to limit exposure to drift. If you need help selecting the right herbicide or understanding application rates and rules, contact your local extension agent.

Smooth sumac shows its brilliant fall color in Missouri, where prairie intermingles with oak-hickory woodland.

WEEDING AND MULCHING
continued

Permeable landscape fabric is one of the best physical weed controls in groundcover beds. Roll the fabric over the bed; hold it in place with landscape pins. Cut slits to plant through. After planting, hide the fabric under a layer of mulch.

MULCHING YOUNG PLANTINGS

Mulching is invaluable for new plantings. It suppresses weeds by preventing light from reaching the soil surface. Weeds that do break through the mulch are easy to spot and usually easy to pull. A layer of mulch maintains moisture in the soil near the groundcover's roots and keeps soil cool in summer. Organic mulches enrich soil with humus and nutrients as they decompose.

Apply mulch in spring after the soil has warmed, spreading it thickly and evenly. To aid plant growth, spread fertilizer over the bed before mulching or mix the recommended amount into the mulch.

In cold climates, cover new plantings, especially fall-planted ones, with a winter mulch to protect them from freezing. Spread the mulch before the first hard freeze. This keeps the ground warm and gives fall-planted groundcovers more time to establish before winter arrives.

The greatest risk to established plants in winter is not the freezing but the soil thawing and refreezing. For established groundcovers, apply the mulch after the ground has frozen. Mulched soil is more likely to stay frozen and keep plants dormant even during warm spells.

Winter mulch materials include pine needles and evergreen boughs. Apply a loose, 4- to 6-inch-deep layer over the plants. This insulates the plants and protects them from cold, dry winter wind. Don't apply mulch so thick that it mats and smothers plants.

MULCHES

Here are a few of the many organic materials available for mulching.

WOOD PRODUCTS: Chipped or shredded bark—usually fir, pine, or redwood—makes an excellent, attractive mulch. Its texture ranges from fine to coarse. Bark chips and shredded bark are readily available in small bags or in bulk. They may be more expensive than other mulches, but they are long-lasting. The size of the chips to use depends on availability and personal taste. Large chips allow more air and water movement through the soil because they don't mat against the soil surface. They also let in more light, so weed seeds can germinate. Smaller chips may work better around low-growing groundcovers or ones with finely textured foliage because they readily filter through the leaves. Sawdust is inexpensive; in some areas, you can even get it for free. But it is not as attractive as bark products, and it tends to tie up the nitrogen in the soil as microbes break the sawdust down. If you use sawdust, buy a product that is fortified with nitrogen, or add additional nitrogen to your beds at a rate of one half pound per 100 square feet of fresh sawdust mulch. Apply sawdust mulch 1 inch deep.

PINE NEEDLES: Pine needles—also called pine straw—are readily available in some regions and are very attractive. They can be expensive if bought in bales; free pine straw may be available from your own yard or from neighbors. Pine-needle mulches last for several years and are ideal for groundcovers that prefer acid soil, such as azaleas.

STRAW, HAY, AND GRASS CLIPPINGS: These readily available mulches are effective and free, but they are less attractive than pine bark and needles. They degrade rapidly, so you must replenish them frequently. Their coarse texture makes them troublesome to apply at even depths because they mound up easily, and they often contain weed seeds.

TREE LEAVES: Leaves are free and readily available. Collect them from your yard as you rake in autumn. They tend to degrade rapidly and blow about, so heavy, thick leaves work best. Shredded leaves stay in place better and are more aesthetic as well.

Heavy, coarse-textured leaves, such as oak leaves, typically provide a looser mulch than light leaves, such as from maples, which tend to mat down. For that reason, heavy, coarse-textured leaves make a good winter mulch. To use lighter-weight leaves, shred or chop them so they will be less likely to blow around.

COMPOSTED MANURE: This is a rich source of nutrients and is often easy to obtain. You can sometimes get it free from local stables and farms. Processed or composted bagged manure is available from retail outlets.

Fresh manure is high in salts and nutrients that can burn plants. It may also contain grass and weed seeds, which will germinate in your beds. Make sure stable manure is properly composted, not just aged. Proper composting, in which the pile heats up to at least 160° F, kills weed seeds. Packaged, processed manure is usually seed free. Even though processed, it can be high in salts. Manure mulches must be replenished about once a year.

NEWSPAPER PRODUCTS: Old newspapers are effective, cheap, and readily available. They are excellent for suppressing weeds and retaining moisture in the soil, but they are unattractive and, when wet, can mat around plants. They last only one season. Save papers at your house and lay them in sheets around plants, or shred them for fluffier mulch.

A new product, which currently has limited regional distribution, is newspaper processed into nuggets. It is more attractive than homemade newspaper mulches.

You can also improve aesthetics by laying sheets of newspaper around plants and covering them with another mulch, such as bark chips. Not only will it look better, you will be adding organic matter to the area.

ORGANIC BYPRODUCTS: Corncobs, mushroom compost, peanut or pecan hulls, cotton-gin trash, waste sludge, and many other byproducts of agriculture and industry are excellent mulches and may be available for free or for a small fee in your area. These mulches vary in nutrient and organic matter content but are quite attractive and effective, as well as long-lived in the landscape. Check your local sources of these products.

COCOA HULLS: This speciality mulch has a delicious scent when fresh, and it is an excellent source of potassium. However, cocoa hulls mulch can be expensive, and it may mold in wet situations. Also, cocoa is believed to be toxic to pets.

Fine shredded bark

Coarse shredded bark

Cocoa hulls

Compost

Leaf mold

Pine straw

THUGS OF NATURAL LANDSCAPES: INVASIVE PLANTS

Native to Europe and Asia, purple loosestrife is an invasive perennial in North America.

Invasive plants are plants that, once introduced into new areas free from their natural competitors, are able to proliferate and persist to the detriment of the existing plants and animals. Invasive plants can cause widespread harm to the environment, the economy, and human health. Plants that are invasive in one locale may be well-behaved in another area.

In their native habitats, plants we call invasive are quite often found in small, well-behaved populations. This is because they occur with other organisms that keep them in balance. It is not until the species are removed from this in-balance habitat that their invasive characters emerge.

Unchecked by competitors, invasives grow and reproduce. Thick growths of nonnative weeds can displace the native plants that once provided food and shelter for the native animals. As the population of an invasive plant rises, populations of other plants and animals fall. Some weeds even change the character of the entire habitat by altering processes like fire, nutrient flow, and flooding.

Protecting natural landscapes from invasives is more than a feel-good measure. Invasives lead to the extinction of endangered plants and animals, and they cost money. By impacting agriculture, forestry, and fisheries, invasives cost the U.S. economy $137 billion a year, according to the Nature Conservancy.

WHAT CAN YOU DO?

Pay attention to the plants you're growing, and ask for only noninvasive species when acquiring new plants. It is entirely possible that an unassuming plant in your garden is, without your knowledge, establishing an invasive population outside your garden.

Never dispose of aquarium plants by dropping them into waterways and only buy weed-free, composted soil amendments for your garden.

Avoid plants that self-seed and thus disperse seedlings that may come up in unexpected places outside your garden. Plants that produce many seeds and just keep coming back even when you try to remove them are also potentially invasive. Don't plant or encourage weedy volunteers that appear in parks or abandoned lots. Work toward and promote landscape designs that are friendly to regional ecosystems.

Seek information on which species are invasive in your area and remove plants that are recognized problems. Check with botanical gardens, horticulturists, conservationists, and government agencies.

Prevent landscape disturbance. Invasives will thrive in bare soil or tilled earth where native plants have been displaced. One key to controlling invasives is to protect healthy plant communities.

If your natural landscape includes a meadow, mow it at least once a year. Regularly walk your entire property and eliminate invasive plants. If you find them while they're still small, they are much easier to remove and eliminate. Use herbicides if necessary, but only with the guidance of a licensed applicator.

After removing invasives it is important to replant. Invasive plants exploit bare soil and unused niches. If you remove a weed, the invasive plant will come right back unless you substitute another plant.

ELEVEN INVASIVE PLANTS

Name	Where It's a Problem	How Does It Spread?	Chief Problem Caused	What to Do
Porcelainberry *Ampelopsis brevipedunculata*	Northeast, North, East Coast	Seeds fall in disturbed soil. Widely available from nurseries.	Rapid vine growth outcompetes and shades out native plants.	Cut back in spring to reduce flowering. Treat stumps with herbicide
Giant reed *Arundo donax*	California, Southwest, upper South	Stem fragments float, take root, and initiate new infestations.	Chokes streams, increases fire potential, and reduces wildlife habitat.	Difficult: prescribed burning, herbicides, or both. Check with expert.
Oriental bittersweet *Celastrus orbiculatus*	New York to North Carolina, west to Illinois	Seeds spread by birds; also has creeping stems and root suckers.	Threatens forested and open areas where it grows over and kills other plants.	Pull out by roots before fruiting. Use herbicides such as glyphosate.
Russian olive *Elaeagnus angustifolia*	Eastern, central, and western U.S.	Primarily seeds are eaten and spread by birds.	Outcompetes natives, interferes with plant succession, and depletes water reserves.	Cut down and remove.
Cogon grass *Imperata cylindrica*	South and southeastern U.S., to east Texas	Plants produce several thousand tiny seeds and tough rhizomes.	Displaces native species with a dense mat of flammable thatch and leaves.	Mow in late spring and spray 6" sprouts with glyphosate. Also spray in fall before frost.
Bush honeysuckle *Lonicera* species	Central Great Plains to southern New England	More than 20 birds feed on fruits and spread seeds.	Rapidly invades, forming a dense layer that crowds and shades out natives.	Pull seedlings by root. Cut large plants to ground, treat stumps with glyphosate.
Purple loosestrife *Lythrum salicaria*	All states except Florida	Fast growth; spreads via root and stem segments and seeds.	Destroys thousands of acres of open-water habitat.	Remove small populations by hand. Only biocontrol—a beetle—can control large populations.
Fountain grass *Pennisetum setaceum*	Arizona, California, Colorado, Hawaii, Florida, Louisiana, and Tennessee	Perennial grass that produces long-lived seeds.	Aggressive, fire-adapted colonizer out-competes native plants and rapidly reestablishes after burning.	Destroy flowers to prevent seeds; remove plants by hand; use systemic herbicides such as glyphosate.
Japanese knotweed *Polygonum cuspidatum*	Maine to Wisconsin, south to Louisiana; some Midwest and Western states	Spreads by rhizomes and seeds, often in topsoil.	Forms dense, persistent thickets that exclude native vegetation and alter natural ecosystems, especially near streams.	Remove plants including roots and runners. Treat cut stumps and leaves with herbicide.
Common buckthorn *Rhamnus cathartica*	Eastern Canada, south to Missouri and east to New England	Plentiful fruit is eaten and spread by birds and mice.	Forms dense thickets, crowding out native shrubs and herbs.	Uproot and dispose of plants. Use herbicides to destroy thickets.
Multiflora rose *Rosa multiflora*	Midwest and Northeast	Birds, especially cedar waxwing and American robin, distribute seeds.	Fast and prolific growth creates impenetrable thickets.	Cut and then apply herbicide to stumps.

ENCOURAGING WILDLIFE

Toads, like this one pausing near a foam flower (Tiarella), help control garden pests.

One of the great joys of having a natural garden is observing the wildlife it attracts. The creatures may be as small as insects or as large as deer. Learning to attract the wildlife you want while moderating damage other wildlife may cause will make natural gardening more delightful.

Environmental communities include a great variety of living creatures. An average suburban lawn may be home to dozens of species of insects, although many are minuscule. A meadow contains even more. The less you maintain your garden, the greater the diversity you encourage, which provides a wide opportunity for observing and enjoying the richness of the garden. Although they eat holes in the leaves of plants, some caterpillars are attractive and fascinating to observe with their brightly colored bristles. They contribute interest and beauty as well as food for birds, and, after their pupal stage, they become attractive butterflies.

Your garden soil, the plants growing in it, and the litter on its surface all teem with a multitude of organisms. Although many are microscopic, they have a profound effect on the life of larger plants and animals. They are an integral part of the biological community. Much of this microscopic life eats discarded plant and animal parts, which become food for animals and birds. The wise gardener supports these microorganisms by providing plenty of organic matter for them to recycle.

This ruby-throated hummingbird nest is masterfully camouflaged with bits of lichen bound with spiderweb.

The gulf fritillary larva lives on leaves of passionflower (Passiflora). Butterfly names that include a plant reference are clues to the caterpillar's diet: Pipevine swallowtail, spicebush swallowtail, and cabbage white butterfly all feed on their namesake plants.

BIRDS

One of the key benefits of a natural landscape is that birds will love it. A garden full of birds is a constant fascination to children and adults alike. The songs of birds and their activities are captivating attractions.

BIRDS ARE ALSO USEFUL: They eat a large variety and quantity of insects. Each day, swallows eat their weight in insects, including mosquitoes. Birds are among the best natural means of keeping garden pests in check.

More species of birds, as well as other wildlife, live in the transitional zone, between deep forest and meadow than in any other area. This transition zone, called an edge, where shrubs and small trees begin, is an important source of shelter. Ground-feeding birds that have ventured into an open meadow can dash under the shrubs for protection when they see the hawk's shadow. Edges also have abundant food for a wide variety of songbirds. Birds that live in the deep forest visit its edges but are rarely seen in the urban or suburban garden.

BASIC NEEDS: Like all living things, birds seek an environment that provides the basics: food, water, shelter, and a place to rear their young. The key to attracting birds to your garden is to create—or help nature create—an environment that provides these four basic needs.

Water is the essential element for survival. Most animal species cannot live for long without a clean and plentiful supply of water. An old wine barrel, a plastic bowl, a commercially made birdbath, a garden fountain, or a pond will all make water accessible to wildlife. Water should be available during all seasons of the year. In the North or in the mountains, where hard freezes occur, a small immersion heater will keep a pond or a birdbath from icing over.

BIRDS NEED SHALLOW WATER: A container with a gently sloping bottom is best. If you build a pond in your garden, create a shallow edge area where birds can bathe, or give them a separate, shallow birdbath with its bowl elevated to provide some safety from house cats and other predators. The water should be as clean and free from toxic substances as possible. Keep insecticides well away from the pond and the birdbath.

Different species of birds have very different feeding habits. Insects are the primary source of food for robins, swallows, flycatchers, vireos, warblers, and woodpeckers, which frequent

woodland meadows and their edges. Some bird species are grain eaters and are attracted to seed-bearing grasses and bird feeders. Other birds prefer berries, nuts, and fruit and are attracted to gardens with fruiting plants. Still other birds are not highly specialized in their dietary needs and eat a variety of foods. For example, hummingbirds will supplement their diet of flower nectar with insects.

Nectar-generous shrubs add up to hummingbird heaven: orange cape fuchsia (Phygelius capensis), red Salvia greggii, and purple butterfly bush (Buddleia).

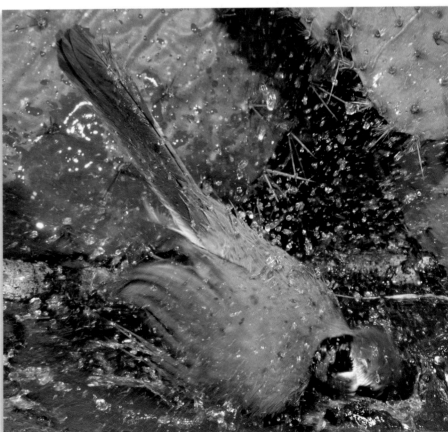

The brilliantly colored green jay is a tropical bird that is common to the lower Rio Grande Valley. It visits area garden feeders in winter.

BIRDS
continued

Trees, shrubs, vines, perennials, and grasses that bear seeds, nuts, and fruit supply wildlife with essential edibles and nesting materials.

BIRD FEEDERS: You can do more to invite birds into your garden by supplying them with food year-round, via bird feeders. When birds become aware that there is always an ample supply of food, they will add your yard to their schedule of daily rounds. Birds are often at their most colorful during spring and summer, another reason for inviting them into your yard throughout the year. They may well choose your land to nest and raise their young, and young birds often return to where they hatched and learned to fly, especially when conditions are welcoming.

To attract a wide variety of birds, offer a variety of food and feeding stations. Ground-feeding birds, such as quail, need feeding locations at ground level. Some ground feeders prefer slightly raised platforms. If hawks are prevalent in your area, provide these feeding stations with a wire roof; the birds will be protected from predators but you will still be able to observe them.

Some birds spend little time on the ground and have a strong preference for raised feeders. You can hang them on tree trunks or long raised poles or suspend them from a tree branch or porch beam. Place them in locations that can be reached easily for refilling, or fasten them to a pulley so that you can raise and lower them. To protect birds from predators—such as house cats—hang the feeder on a slim cable or rope that cats cannot climb. In addition, make sure that the feeder is far enough away from tree trunks or branches that predators can't jump to it.

Freestanding feeders should be mounted on smooth, metal-clad poles, which will also keep squirrels from stealing seeds from the birds.

Another way to keep squirrels from raiding the bird feeder is to provide them with their own feeding area. They're fond of corn, so you could build them a special corn feeder. Drive long nails

Plants attract birds by providing food. An eastern bluebird (left) has picked a mountain ash (Sorbus) berry. This red-bellied woodpecker (above) feeds on suet provided by a gardener.

This northern oriole is browsing through a basket of threads and yarn snippets for nesting material.

through a solid board so that the point of the nail extends 2 to 3 inches. Push dried ears of corn onto the protruding nails. Some birds will eat the kernels, too.

To help birds survive the winter cold, offer them high-energy foods in the form of fat and protein. Suet is easily available and a favorite even among birds that are mostly grain eaters. Other sources of fat are bacon drippings, shortening, and cheese. Butter cut into small cubes is attractive to many birds.

To attract hummingbirds to your garden, hang special hummingbird feeders. They come in a variety of shapes and sizes, and they should be colorful—red, orange, or yellow. Fill them with a sugar solution (1 part granulated sugar to 4 parts water). Do not add food coloring; some types produce a rocklike residue in the hummingbird's stomach. Avoid honey too; it can cause a fungus disease that attacks the hummingbird's tongue. Hummingbird feeders should be cleaned every few days with a vinegar solution to prevent harmful fungus buildup.

Many other birds also like sugar water. Position a hummingbird feeder with a convenient perch for birds that don't drink on the wing.

There is an important caution regarding birdfeeders: They can sometimes spread diseases among birds. The solution is to clean birdfeeders on a regular basis.

BIRDHOUSES: In combination with feeders, birdhouses encourage birds to settle in to raise their young.

Making nesting material available will also attract birds to your garden. A natural garden offers sources of nesting material that might not be found in a garden where the grass is mowed regularly and the leaves and twigs are raked and bagged. Birds will also use bits of string or yarn, strips of cloth, cotton filling from old furniture, and even animal hair. Hang a wire basket full of useful materials from a tree, or drape the materials over a clothesline so that they are conspicuous and easy for the birds to gather. Cut stringy materials into 8-inch lengths so they are less likely to snag as the birds fly with them.

Offer different types of birdhouses to attract different species. Purple martins, for example, nest in communities and prefer birdhouses that look like multistory apartments. A large variety of birdhouses and nesting boxes are available through plant nurseries and garden stores. Many pet stores have them too.

BUTTERFLIES

By planting a natural garden that includes diverse kinds of plant materials and avoiding spraying pesticides, you will attract butterflies such as the monarch to your garden.

Monarch butterflies migrate north from central Mexico in spring and return there every fall to spend the winter. This journey extends thousands of miles across the United States and into Canada. It is a saga of the relation-ship between the monarch and the milkweed plant.

On the northbound trip monarchs cannot make the journey in one try. Adult butterflies fly for a week or so, lay their brood eggs on milkweed plants, and then die. Their larvae hatch on the hosts, grow into caterpillars, pupate, and then become adult butterflies, which continue on the next leg of the species' northerly excursion. This incredible journey to Canada requires the development of three or four generations of butterflies.

A mix of flowers at various heights accommodates the habits of many butterflies, from small ones that forage low to high-fliers such as swallowtails.

In fall the migration is reversed, except that some of the adult monarchs do make the entire trip back to central Mexico, traveling for three months or more to their ancestral home. They return unerringly to cluster in groups of millions during the mild southern winters.

Without milkweed the story of their migration would not be told. In your natural garden, a patch of milkweed will help keep the story alive for future generations.

BUTTERFLY PLANTS: Flowers and butterflies belong together. The best way to attract butterflies is to plant the flowers they prefer. Many garden flowers will attract butterflies, allowing you to enjoy these colorful insects as they float and flutter from plant to plant.

A monarch butterfly sips nectar from a milkweed flower (top), while a larva feeds on milkweed leaves.

Butterfly plants are available in wide variety, from annuals and perennials to large shrubs and even some trees.

Butterflies begin their life as clusters of eggs on host plants. As does the monarch, some butterflies require specific host plants. The eggs hatch into small larvae that can grow into very large caterpillars. These caterpillars eat heartily of their preferred food, thus reducing some garden leaves to bare skeletons.

When ready, each caterpillar pupates into a chrysalis. Most pupae stay in this stage for only a week or two; some species, such as swallowtails, pupate through the winter. When a butterfly emerges from a chrysalis, it is full grown and ready to mate and lay more eggs. Some species of butterflies live for only a few days. Others live for nearly a year.

Butterflies are cold-blooded and require an air temperature of at least 60° F in order to fly, so you won't see them flitting in the garden on cool spring mornings. Most butterflies sip flower nectar exclusively; some—such as the mourning cloak, red admiral, and viceroy—eat rotting fruit as their primary source of food. For these butterflies, set out diced apple, banana, and pear in a solution of molasses water, which hastens fermentation.

The flowers that produce the nectar loved by most butterflies and hummingbirds are

often the ones gardeners consider the most beautiful because of their appearance or fragrance. In addition, many favorite shrubs and vines are attractive to butterflies, including azalea, honeysuckle, lantana, lilac, milkweed, rabbitbrush, viburnum, and wisteria.

Another way to attract butterflies is to provide host plants for the eggs and caterpillars. Some butterflies are named for the plants that host them. The spicebush swallowtail is hosted by spicebush (*Lindera benzoin*). The European cabbage butterfly prefers members of the cabbage family. Other specific butterfly-plant relationships include the orange sulfur butterfly with alfalfa, the black swallowtail and the anise swallowtail with Queen Anne's lace and parsley, and the painted lady with hibiscus and mallow. The larvae of these butterflies will usually leave other garden plants untouched.

BUTTERFLY FEEDERS: The same solution used in hummingbird feeders—1 part granulated sugar to 4 parts water—will attract butterflies. A simple butterfly feeder can be made by saturating some absorbent material, such as tissue paper, with the sugar solution and placing it in a shallow dish. Or to give the butterflies something to perch on while drinking, place several plastic kitchen scouring pads in a bowl of the same solution.

BUTTERFLY SHELTERS: You can build a shelter for butterflies that fits right into your natural garden setting. A butterfly log pile provides a comfortable sanctuary for perching, as well as a safe haven for hibernating. A log pile is a much more effective butterfly haven than the commercially available butterfly houses that may be purchased. Butterflies like cavities, so the spaces between the logs are a natural place for them to congregate. Many creatures besides butterflies will also find shelter in this pile.

Start with about four logs 5 to 6 inches in diameter and 4 to 5 feet long. Lay them side by side but separated by a few inches. Then place another layer of logs across this base. Lay five or six layers; then place roofing material or a waterproof tarpaulin across the top layer of logs to protect the butterflies from the rain. Add another layer of logs over the roofing material to hide it and hold it in place.

Butterflies are attracted to shallow water. If you build a pond in your garden, make one edge shallow and adjoining some garden soil that will remain wet or muddy. Butterflies can drink there as well as take in other vital nutrients. Sprinkle a little salt on the muddy section from time to time to provide butterflies with sodium. Because excessive salt can damage plants, use it sparingly.

Butterflies need warmth in order to function. Place some flat stones in a sunny location so the butterflies in the garden will have a basking platform to warm themselves on a sunny morning. Locating a few of their favorite plants nearby makes the butterfly garden complete.

Hackberry and red-spotted purple butterflies (top) are attracted to fruit. Lilac flowers provide nectar for the common buckeye (above) and other early-spring arrivals.

Openings among a pile of stacked logs provide inviting places for butterflies to seek shelter from the elements. A waterproof roof, camouflaged by a final layer of logs, keeps the interior dry.

OTHER INSECTS

Even diminutive ponds attract dragonflies, which in turn feed on pests.

Encouraging insects to live in your garden may seem contradictory to experienced gardeners. It is true that some insects are destructive when they become too numerous, but, in general, insects are a positive influence in the garden. Bees, butterflies, and wasps are necessary for pollination. Many of them are beautiful too.

Bumblebees, along with other native wild bees, provided most flower pollination in North America before the arrival of the honeybee from Europe. Wild bees are faster and more efficient pollinators than honeybees because they do not gather nectar and pollen for long-term storage. Wild bee hives do not live through the winter. Only the queen survives, creating a new nest in spring.

In most situations we can trust nature to keep pest and predator cycles within a reasonable balance. When pest populations grow rapidly, predator populations lag just a little behind. When predators have eaten most of the pests, they themselves succumb to lack of food. This allows the pest population to begin another growth cycle. And so it goes.

Most insects are neither harmful nor beneficial to garden plants. Many species of

Healthy gardens include spiders, which trap and consume many pests, such as mosquitoes and small flies.

wildlife depend on insects for food. Bats live on insects. Shrews and voles are insectivores. Many birds eat insects as an important part of their diet. Raccoons and opossums are omnivores, with insects constituting a large part of their diet. Reptiles—and frogs, toads, and other amphibians—depend on insects. A standing dead tree attracts wood borers— and woodpeckers, which consider the borers a delicacy. Ponds attract insects, which in turn provide food for fish and frogs.

Many insects are effective predators. Ladybugs prey on aphids. A diversity of plants will sustain enough aphids to maintain a watchful supply of predators. With a sufficient variety of plants, there is little chance of a major epidemic.

Wasps and hornets are effective and efficient garden predators. White-faced hornets kill horseflies and eat them with dispatch. Yellow jackets, a type of paper wasp, are exceptionally good at controlling striped cucumber beetles and other chewing insects.

Among the most interesting and spectacular of the predatory insects are the dragonfly and the praying mantis, or mantid. Large mantids will even eat mice, small snakes, and other mantids. Crickets and grasshoppers are related to mantids. Tree crickets are vegetarians in their youth but as adults eat aphids and garden grubs. Spiders also prey on insects.

Aphids and ants are paired in an interesting relationship that protects your plants from other insects. Each day, aphids process plant fluid many times their body weight. The excess fluids are excreted as a sweet sugar solution called honeydew, a favorite food for ants. Ants protect this food supply even to the extent of driving away or killing caterpillars and other insects that might interfere with the aphids. Although aphids harm plants, this relationship with the ants does have its benefits.

Many millions of insects exist in nature, many of them not even classified yet. Heroic methods to destroy garden pests may do serious, unanticipated damage to not yet fully understood parts of the delicate web of life.

All of this does not mean, that we should avoid controlling garden pests. When severe infestations occur, there is a need for specifically targeted action. If you have a garden insect you don't recognize, visit your local nursery. Chances are the staff can identify the insect and recommend a solution. However, often the best solution is patience in your working association with nature.

EARTHWORMS

Healthy garden soil is dependent on earthworms. As they burrow into the soil, they aerate it. They eat decomposing organic matter and carry it into the topsoil, fertilizing the soil as the food passes through their digestive systems. Soil made healthy by earthworms will support the myriad other life forms necessary for vigorous plant growth.

Earthworms also help recycle organic matter in a compost pile. In fact, they will reduce the need to turn the pile to keep it aerated, which facilitates the process of decomposition.

If you don't have room for a compost pile, you can build a small earthworm composter, either in the house or, in mild winter climates, outside. Select a lidded, rectangular plastic storage container that holds about 10 gallons. Place it on a waterproof tray to catch any surplus moisture. Drill eight drainage holes approximately ¼ inch in diameter in the bottom and another eight ventilation holes through the sides of the container, near the top.

Fill the container to within 4 inches of the top with bedding material of moist potting soil or thoroughly dampened peat moss. Add a pound (from 1,000 to 2,000 worms) of red wiggler worms (*Eisenia foetida*) to the container. Red wigglers, also sold as compost worms or fish worms, are available from garden nurseries and bait stores or through the mail from one of the sources listed on page 93.

The presence of earthworms in your garden soil is an indication of good soil health.

Earthworms daily process organic material equal to about one half their body weight. To feed them, place kitchen food scraps, including coffee grounds and all vegetable material (not animal or dairy products), under the surface of the bedding soil in the composter, in a different location each day. Eggshells are beneficial (pulverize them first); the calcium in the shells helps prevent the bedding from becoming too acidic. Cover the surface of the bedding material with a few layers of damp newspaper.

Empty the composter every ten to twelve weeks; then place new bedding in the container. The composted material can be used as a rich mulch in the garden or mixed with potting soil for container plants. Half the earthworms should be separated from the old bedding and returned to the earthworm composter. The other half can be placed in the garden under some moist mulch material, added to an old compost pile, or shared with a friend.

Home composting systems vary from simple to elaborate. This design makes turning piles easy and access to finished compost convenient.

MAMMALS

Depending on where you live, mammals in your garden can range in size from the tiniest shrew to a moose weighing over a thousand pounds. Most, especially the smaller ones, are welcome most of the time.

Mammals are endlessly amusing to watch. Raccoons, with their black bandit's mask, are guileless entertainers. The acrobatics of squirrels can captivate for hours. The gamboling antics of young white-tailed deer playing in a meadow delight people of all ages. And the flight ballet of bats can keep audiences spellbound while the bats are visible at dusk.

Mammals play an important role in keeping nature's balance in the garden. A few bats zig-zagging overhead consume thousands of mosquitoes and other flying insects each evening. Not always seen but equally important are moles, voles, and shrews. Eastern moles forage on grubs and bugs that live underground. Shrews eat insects that inhabit the surface of the ground; in fact shrews are ferocious and will eat small rodents such as mice and infant rats.

Foxes, coyotes, and house cats keep small rodents in check. Skunks eat grubs, beetles, and rodents and sometimes share outdoor milk bowls with house cats.

Entice squirrels away from bird feeders by providing them with their own food. Dried corn—these cobs are supported by nails— is preferred.

ATTRACTING MAMMALS

Small rodents, such as voles and shrews, are the most numerous mammals in the garden, but due to their diminutive size and shyness, they are not frequently seen. The most visible mammals in North American gardens are squirrels, of which the most common is the gray squirrel. There are more per acre in urban areas than in rural settings. These animals prefer large-canopy trees but are also at home in a small woodland.

Nest boxes, similar to large birdhouses, will attract squirrels into small-canopy trees, particularly if food is provided. Squirrel feeders are commercially available. Some of them are cleverly designed to require squirrels to perform for their dinner.

Chipmunks are small, engaging animals that adapt readily to the natural garden. Wood piles, log structures such as the one described for butterflies, and brush piles are good nesting places. Because chipmunks are very nearsighted, they are easy prey for house cats. If you or your neighbors have cats, the survival of chipmunks within the cats' hunting territory is questionable. Attaching a bell to a cat's collar might save the life of a chipmunk or a ground-feeding bird.

Encourage chipmunks by providing hiding places. Discourage them by blocking or eliminating their hideouts or by enlisting a willing cat.

Raccoons nest almost anywhere that offers shelter. A hollow log or a box with a waterproof top in the crotch of a tree will provide a home. Because well-fed raccoons eventually grow quite large, make sure that the box is solidly supported and securely attached to the tree. An alternative is to affix the box to a post in the ground so that the height of the box matches that of a substantial tree limb.

Make a simple raccoon nesting box from plywood. Make it 16 inches square and 4 feet tall. A simple sloping shed roof keeps out the rain. The entrance is a 6-inch-diameter hole near the top of one side. Hinge one of the sides to allow the box to be opened for cleaning. One sheet of plywood (use ⅝-inch exterior grade) will make a nesting box with enough wood left over for a birdhouse.

You can use the same idea to build a nesting box for squirrels. It should be 8 inches square and about 20 inches tall. The access hole (make it 3 inches in diameter) should also be near the top. Set the squirrel nesting box at least 10 feet above the ground.

Mammals are finicky about where they nest. A box you provide may be occupied immediately by the animal you meant it for, or it may stay empty for years or attract other tenants altogether.

Planting shrubs and trees that produce berries, fruit, and nuts will attract mammals to the garden. So will feeders. A simple, sturdy tray with a roof to help keep the food supply dry will serve as a squirrel feeder. Squirrels are fond of corn, which is less expensive than most birdseed and may keep them out of the bird feeder, where they tend to eat voraciously.

Raccoons are fond of table scraps such as meat, vegetable, and fruit trimmings. Put out the food in the same place and at the same time in the evening; raccoons will be waiting nearby. A simple flat stone in the garden or a flat board attached to a fence top will do for a feeding platform. Provide fresh water nearby; if water is available, raccoons will wash their food before eating it. Resist the temptation to feed raccoons, or any wild animal, by hand. Raccoons are unpredictable and exceptionally strong for their size, and they have very sharp teeth and claws. Locate raccoon feeding platforms in plain view, away from the house.

A muddy beach at the edge of a garden pond is a typical feeding site for a raccoon.

MANAGING MAMMALS

Rabbits often work from the bottom to the top of a plant and may prefer the side of a plant or garden that is closer to shelter. They usually leave behind clusters of dark brown pellets.

A cylinder of hardware cloth around the base of a young tree protects its tender bark from rabbits. Be sure to remove the wire before it chokes the growing trunk.

One rabbit in the vegetable patch is a cute visitor, but ten of them will eat all the lettuce. They can do more serious damage too. A fluffy cottontail could strip the bark from the base of a fruit tree, killing it. Mice and voles also eat the bark of fruit trees.

This potential problem is easy to solve. Make a cylinder of hardware cloth (a galvanized wire mesh with ¼-inch holes) to circle the trunk, allowing for at least a ½-inch space between the wire and the tree. The cylinder should be at least 16 inches tall to protect the tree against rabbits standing on their hind legs.

Although a family of raccoons can be a delight when they are gathered at the feeder and disposing of kitchen scraps, they can become a nuisance when they break into garbage receptacles or raid compost piles. They may also spread bits of refuse throughout the yard. Strap down your garbage can lid with a bungee cord hooked to the handles on each side, or buy a sturdy, animal-proof composter for domestic garbage.

Because composting is an important part of maintaining a natural garden and because compost piles attract animals, a commercially made garbage composter is a good investment. Many are constructed of strong, high-impact hard plastic and will resist animals as clever and persistent as urban raccoons or coyotes.

Groundhogs, also called woodchucks, are herbivores that can be a nuisance in a vegetable garden. Keep them out with wire fencing about 30 inches high, plus 8 inches buried in the ground to keep the critters from burrowing under the fence.

KEEP WILD ANIMALS WILD: Don't allow animals or birds to build nests in structures housing humans. Raccoons and squirrels like to nest in chimneys and attics. They are capable of stripping the insulation off electrical wiring, which creates a fire hazard. Close holes into attics or garage roofs, and don't let birds or animals nest in toolsheds. Birds can carry human diseases so don't let them nest near where humans dwell.

If you do find animal or bird nests in structures you use or live in, call the health department for advice rather than attempting to remove the nests yourself. When cleaning up dried mouse or rat droppings, first spray them with a fine water mist and wear a respirator or high-quality dust mask.

Deer can do as much damage in a natural meadow as in a garden. When deer populations exceed 18 animals per square mile in natural environments, the pressure

Delightful visitors on the one hand, deer also like to eat many kinds of plants and thus cause problems for gardeners. The gardener's best defense is a strong fence.

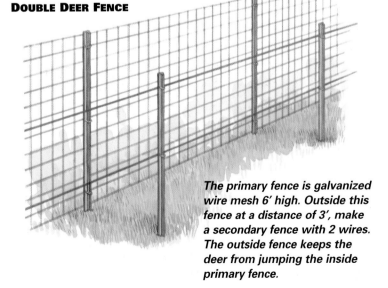

Groundhogs often knock down large plants to reach the flower buds and succulent tips they prefer.

of their feeding begins to eliminate some of the plant species native to the site.

In areas with very high deer populations, the only practical way to protect flower and vegetable gardens is with a high, open wire fence or a double fence. (Deer can clear an 8-foot-high fence with relative ease.) A double fence consists of an inner fence at least 6 feet tall built with solid posts and galvanized wire mesh and an outer fence about 3 feet away and consisting of a pair of horizontal wires, one 30 inches above the ground and the other about 5 feet above the ground. This arrangement alters the jump pattern of deer and will keep most of them out of the garden while still allowing you to see them browse around the garden through the open mesh.

What about rabies? In some parts of the United States and Canada, rabies has become a serious problem in the wildlife population. Rabies is transmitted in saliva. Rabid foxes, skunks, raccoons, and bears have appeared in some northeastern cities and suburbs. Animals with rabies sometimes seem lost and confused. Animal lovers are often tempted to help, particularly if the animal is small and in the garden. However, it is best to call an animal control agency instead of trying to help the animal yourself.

The actual incidence of rabies among humans is very small, but the treatment for this dangerous disease is an ordeal. Domestic animals in high-incidence areas should be vaccinated. Some people fear that bats may be carriers. Bats, however, do not attack humans; in fact, the teeth of small bats, such as the common brown bat, cannot pierce human skin.

DOUBLE DEER FENCE

The primary fence is galvanized wire mesh 6' high. Outside this fence at a distance of 3', make a secondary fence with 2 wires. The outside fence keeps the deer from jumping the inside primary fence.

USDA Plant Hardiness Zone Map

This map of climate zones helps you select plants for your garden that will survive a typical winter in your region. The United States Department of Agriculture (USDA) developed the map, basing the zones on the lowest recorded temperatures across North America. Zone 1 is the coldest area and Zone 11 is the warmest.

Plants are classified by the coldest temperature and zone they can endure. For example, plants hardy to Zone 6 survive where winter temperatures drop to –10° F. Those hardy to Zone 8 die long before it's that cold. These plants may grow in colder regions but must be replaced each year. Plants rated for a range of hardiness zones can usually survive winter in the coldest region as well as tolerate the summer heat of the warmest one.

To find your hardiness zone, note the approximate location of your community on the map, then match the color band marking that area to the key.

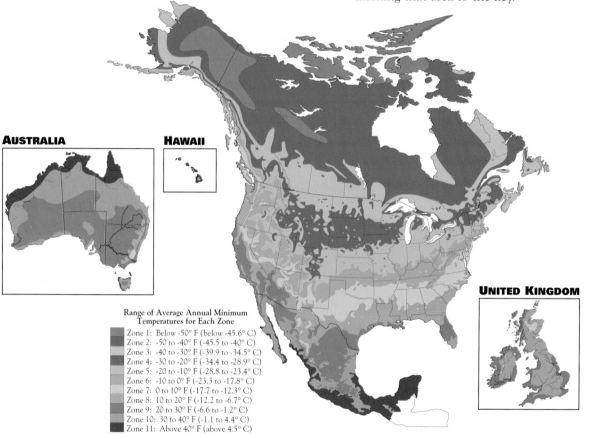

AUSTRALIA

HAWAII

UNITED KINGDOM

Range of Average Annual Minimum
Temperatures for Each Zone

Zone 1: Below -50° F (below -45.6° C)
Zone 2: -50 to -40° F (-45.5 to -40° C)
Zone 3: -40 to -30° F (-39.9 to -34.5° C)
Zone 4: -30 to -20° F (-34.4 to -28.9° C)
Zone 5: -20 to -10° F (-28.8 to -23.4° C)
Zone 6: -10 to 0° F (-23.3 to -17.8° C)
Zone 7: 0 to 10° F (-17.7 to -12.3° C)
Zone 8: 10 to 20° F (-12.2 to -6.7° C)
Zone 9: 20 to 30° F (-6.6 to -1.2° C)
Zone 10: 30 to 40° F (-1.1 to 4.4° C)
Zone 11: Above 40° F (above 4.5° C)

METRIC CONVERSIONS

U.S. Units to Metric Equivalents			Metric Units to U.S. Equivalents		
To Convert From	Multiply By	To Get	To Convert From	Multiply By	To Get
Inches	25.4	Millimeters	Millimeters	0.0394	Inches
Inches	2.54	Centimeters	Centimeters	0.3937	Inches
Feet	30.48	Centimeters	Centimeters	0.0328	Feet
Feet	0.3048	Meters	Meters	3.2808	Feet
Yards	0.9144	Meters	Meters	1.0936	Yards

To convert from degrees Fahrenheit (F) to degrees Celsius (C), first subtract 32, then multiply by .555.

To convert from degrees Celsius to degrees Fahrenheit, multiply by 1.8, then add 32.

RESOURCES

MAIL-ORDER SOURCES OF NATIVE PLANTS

Bamert Seed Co.
1897 County Road 1018
Muleshoe, TX 79347
800/262-9892
www.bamertseed.com

Bowman's Hill Wildflower Preserve
P.O. Box 685
New Hope, PA 18938
215/862-2924
www.bhwp.org

Great Basin Natives
P.O. Box 114
Holden, UT 84636
435/795-2303
www.greatbasinnatives.com

Holland Wildflower Farm
P.O. Box 328
Elkins, AR 72727
501/643-2622
www.hwildflower.com

Ion Exchange
1878 Old Mission Dr.
Harpers Ferry, IA 52146-7533
800/291-2143
www.ionxchange.com

Johnston Seed Co.
P.O. Box 1392
Enid, OK 73702
800/375-4613
www.johnstonseed.com

Kester's Wild Game Food
Nurseries, Inc.
P.O. Box 516
Omro, WI 54963
920/685-2929
www.kestersnursery.com

Landscape Alternatives, Inc.
1705 St. Albans St.
Roseville, MN 55113-6554
651/488-3142
Catalog $2

Larner Seeds
P.O. Box 407
Bolinas, CA 94924
415/868-9407
www.larnerseeds.com
Catalog $2.50

Morning Sky Greenery
24774 450th Ave.
Hancock, MN 56244
320/392-5282
www.morningskygreenery.com
Catalog $2

Native Gardens
5737 Fisher Lane
Greenback, TN 37742
865/856-0220
www.native-gardens.com

Native Seeds/Search
926 N. 4th Ave.
Tucson, AZ 85705
520/622-5561
www.nativeseeds.org
Catalog $1

Pacific Rim Native Plant Nursery
44305 Old Orchard Rd.
Chilliwack, BC V2R 1A9, Canada
604/792-9279
www.hillkeep.ca

Plants of the Southwest
3095 Agua Fria
Santa Fe, NM 87507
800/788-7333
www.plantsofthesouthwest.com
Catalog $3.50

Prairie Habitats, Inc.
Box 10
Argyle, Manitoba R0C 0B0,
Canada
204/467-9371
www.prairiehabitats.com
Catalog $2

Prairie Moon Nursery
Rt. 3, Box 1633
Winona, MN 55987
507/452-1362
www.prairiemoonnursery.com

Prairie Nursery, Inc.
P.O. Box 306
Westfield, WI 53964
800/476-9453
www.prairienursery.com

Prairie Restorations, Inc.
P.O. Box 327
Princeton, MN 55371
763/389-4342
www.prairieresto.com

Prairie Ridge Nursery
9738 Overland Rd.
Mt. Horeb, WI 53572-2832

608/437-5245
www.prairieridgenursery.com

Sharp Bros. Seed Co., Inc.
396 SW Davis St.-LaDue
Clinton, MO 64735
660/885-7551
www.sharpbro.com

Stock Seed Farms, Inc.
28008 Mill Rd.
Murdock, NE 68407-2350
800/759-1520
www.stockseed.com

Taylor Creek Restoration Nurseries
17921 Smith Rd.
Brodhead, WI 53520
608/897-8641
www.appliedeco.com/tcrn

We-Du Nurseries
2055 Polly Spout Rd.
Marion, NC 28752
828/738-8300
www.we-du.com
Catalog $3

Western Native Seed
P.O. Box 188
Coaldale, CO 81222
719/942-3935
http://westernnativeseed.com

Wetlands Nursery, Inc.
P.O. Box 14553
Saginaw, MI 48601
517/752-3492

Wild Earth Native Plant Nursery
22 Conover St.
Freehold, NJ 07728
732/308-9777
Catalog $2

Wildflower Farm, Inc.
RR 3
Schomberg, ON Canada L0G 1T0
905/859-0286
www.wildflowerfarm.com

Wild Seed, Inc.
P.O. Box 27751
Tempe, AZ 85285
602/276-3536

Wildseed Farms
425 Wildflower Hills
Fredericksburg, TX 78624-3000
800/848-0078
www.wildseedfarms.com

INDEX

Page numbers in *italic* type indicate photographs, illustrations, or information in captions.